# Instructional Rounds in Action

D1264813

# Instructional Rounds
# in Action

JOHN E. ROBERTS

HARVARD EDUCATION PRESS
CAMBRIDGE, MASSACHUSETTS

Copyright © 2012 by the President and Fellows of Harvard College

All rights reserved. No part of this publication may be reproduced or transmitted in any form or by any means, electronic or mechanical, including photocopy, recording, or any information storage and retrieval systems, without permission in writing from the publisher.

Library of Congress Control Number 2012941188

Paperback ISBN 978-1-61250-496-4
Library Edition ISBN 978-1-61250-497-1

Published by Harvard Education Press,
an imprint of the Harvard Education Publishing Group

Harvard Education Press
8 Story Street
Cambridge, MA 02138

Cover Design: Sarah Henderson
The typefaces used in this book are Minion Pro, Myriad Pro, and Fenice.

*To the educators who took the time to share*
*their learning so that others might benefit:*
*while my agreement with the school system*
*does not allow me to name you here,*
*several of you went far beyond my expectations*
*and opened your professional lives to me*
*on a daily basis. Thank you.*

# CONTENTS

Most school reforms ask adults to do things they don't know how to do. The more ambitious the reform, the greater the gap between what educators know how to do and what they need to know to meet the demands of the reform. If the situation were otherwise, then school reform would be a relatively easy matter of simply mobilizing educators' current knowledge in the service of collective goals. But teachers don't have their best practices locked up in classroom closets, ready to deploy when policy makers and leaders order them into action. Likewise, most school leaders aren't intentionally keeping their best leadership practices under wraps until they are threatened by accountability requirements. Most educators are currently working at, or near, the limits of their current knowledge and practice.

School reform, if it works at all, works by systematically increasing the learning capacity of individuals and the organizations in which they work. Indeed, the central problem of American school reform is learning. Students learn best when adults are working and learning at the outer edge of their own practice. Instructional rounds is based on the premise that collective observation and analysis of instructional practice, done routinely and within a disciplined stance that honors evidence and predictive validity, helps individuals, schools, and school systems focus their individual and collective learning toward improved learning for students.

But as John Roberts observes, introducing this relatively straightforward idea into schools is a culturally disruptive practice. American schools, among all the school systems in the industrialized world, are the most deeply hardwired, culturally and structurally, to resist systemic practices of adult learning. The deepest irony of American education is that the institutions that are charged with the main responsibility for learning in our society do the worst job of enabling the learning of the people who work in them. The reasons for this phenomenon have been rehearsed ad nauseam in the literature on the history and sociology of American schools.

At the base level, in the default culture of American schools and in the public mind, teaching is considered a relatively easy, nontechnical, intuitively obvious practice that requires a set of largely unspecified, largely interpersonal skills. The common assumption is that for people who have these skills, the work of teaching is relatively straightforward. In human capital terms, this model operates on the assumption that you select good-enough teachers and put them in classrooms, and over the course of their careers, they depreciate whatever knowledge and skill they entered with until, somewhere near the end of their career, they run out of energy and skill and retire. No other knowledge-based industry or enterprise in American society operates on this premise.

Instructional rounds is disruptive, in the sense that Roberts defines it, because it introduces the powerful countercultural idea that people who work in knowledge-based enterprises should be engaged in continuous learning and improve throughout their careers. Moreover, Roberts contends, educators should be doing so in ways that challenge existing beliefs about what students can learn and, more fundamentally, raise questions about the ways schools participate in the reproduction of social and racial inequality in society. In *Instructional Rounds in Action*, Roberts's analysis of rounds leads us through the detailed processes necessary to use a disruptive practice to reshape the default culture of American schools.

John Roberts has been part of a broad network of educators from universities, schools, and school systems at the leading edge of the development and use of instructional rounds. His special passion is the improvement of learning for poor children of color. A central norm of this network, to which the instructional rounds team at Harvard and I belong, is that we view our own work on instructional rounds as a continuous learning process, rather than a process of teaching people how to implement a fixed design. We view the practitioners with whom we work as coproducers and learning partners rather than clients. And we try, not always successfully, to sustain a culture of candor and challenge in sharing our own learning struggles as part of our work with practitioners. We regard the practice of instructional rounds as never becoming a settled set of routines, but always subject to new levels of challenge and learning.

*Instructional Rounds in Action* is a model of how this continuous learning and improvement works. Roberts is both an analyst and a participant in the work he writes about, which in itself is no small disruption of the traditional academic research paradigm. He is a sympathetic colleague in relation to the practitioners with whom he works. But he is also an unflinching critic of the institutional constraints that get in the way of collective learning and the practices that undermine the espoused goals of equality of opportunity in secondary schools. His conclusions are challenges for the future development of the practice, rather than summative assessments of the "success" or "failure" of the practice. And he models the qualities of reflection in actions that are critical to the improvement of practice in the education sector.

I hope that one day, educators will begin to manifest the highest and best qualities of what it means to be a profession. Practices will be anchored in a solid base of knowledge that can be used to judge the quality of work in schools. Professionals will have clear expectations about the learning that has to occur over the course of their career to meet the challenges that society gives them. Educators will challenge existing beliefs about what students can learn and do. School systems will take responsibility for the selection, induction, and development of human talent in the education sector and for the quality of the practice of people who call themselves educators. A useful starting point for this movement is the simple premise that *professions have practices*. They use these practices to develop norms and commitments to each other about what it means to be a professional. They also use these practices to develop a culture of continuous improvement. And they are willing to assess critically the quality of their own work and that of their colleagues, in light of evidence and in the service of collective improvement over time. With this book, John Roberts makes an important contribution to the process of building an education profession.

*Richard F. Elmore*
*Gregory R. Anrig Professor of Educational Leadership*
*Harvard Graduate School of Education*

# Introduction

If there is one common theme of school reform in America, it's that the nation has been largely unsuccessful at improving whole systems of schools across large cities and regions. This state of affairs has frustrated educators and policy makers since at least the publication of *A Nation at Risk* in 1983. Any successes have typically been limited to temporary, fleeting gains in average student achievement, while excellence remains isolated in pockets of those systems and our nation. This pattern is the most consistent result of school improvement efforts in America over the past thirty years, but the reasons for it remain controversial and constantly shifting beneath the feet of educators. In the meantime, the differences in quality between and within school systems produce huge educational inequalities that disproportionately affect students of color and those from poor families. These observations—and some of the possible reasons for them—were recast for me three years ago during a conversation with an experienced educator named Sofia Uson (not her real name).[1] She was in her first year as a facilitator of a school improvement process called *instructional rounds*, the purpose of which is in part to address the wide differences in instructional practice across thirty-eight high schools in her school system.

I had heard that a school district, which for reasons of anonymity I'll call Lakeside Public Schools throughout the book, was planning a remarkably ambitious effort using the instructional rounds process. I already had a good deal of experience with instructional rounds both as a facilitator of rounds in a high school and teaching it alongside the Harvard Graduate School of Education faculty who had developed the process for educators. But at that point, there had been very little systematic research on how school systems were actually using rounds on their own, and I thought Lakeside might provide an opportunity to learn more about that. By chance, Sofia and I had some mutual acquaintances, and she agreed to talk with me. We talked for nearly two hours at our first meeting, discussing her work and my interest in writing about how Lakeside was using instructional rounds.

For Sofia and her Lakeside colleagues, practicing instructional rounds means focusing on the learning of educators about their instruction, but this learning competes with an exhausting list of problems in places like Lakeside. This book describes how Lakeside began to shift its focus to the problems of adult learning, that is, the professional learning of adults in the school system, since those challenges are brought into sharp relief by instructional rounds. The lesson of Lakeside's experience is straightforward: managing this shift to adult learning really means figuring out which things lead to or support adult learning, even while many other things compete for educators' attention and the system's resources. This means educators have to make collective commitments to solving the problems that have previously prevented adult learning. Said another way, practicing instructional rounds regularly puts pressure on the system and thereby activates previously unidentified or unaddressed problems of adult learning. Solving these problems leads to broader, systemic learning, a necessary precursor to improvements in student performance. Examining these problems will also allow readers to realize the main goals of this book: (1) to understand how a school system has to adapt to make instructional rounds a productive learning experience for educators, and (2) to understand the ways a system adapts the instructional rounds process to help it solve the problems that inevitably arise along the way. One of the assumptions of instructional rounds is that students will learn more only if adults learn more about their practice. My assumption is that real school reform—regardless of whether one practices instructional rounds or some other improvement process—means adopting a set of practices that disrupts the culture of adults and fundamentally shifts the patterns of interaction between them.[2] This is a story about the steps Lakeside took toward doing just that.

It's also important to understand what Lakeside wanted from this book, since this will likely resonate with other school leaders and educators. During that first meeting with Sofia, she quickly redirected the conversation and began to outline the terms of the partnership she envisioned. While the conversation remained friendly, she unequivocally explained that she was only interested in this project if the research would help the Lakeside high schools improve. Most educators have been involved with research that doesn't benefit their systems, and Sofia was wary of such an arrangement. And she was feeling the pressure of her new job in a school system with huge challenges. The Lakeside school district has over fifty thousand students who speak at least seventy-three languages. Some 78 percent of the students are identified as black or Latino, and on average, there is a large percentage-point difference between the proficiency rates of those students and their white peers on the state exams. Sofia knew that instructional rounds would require the system to refocus its efforts in a way that would be entirely new for all the staff, but she also felt pulled in a thousand directions on any given day. It was sometimes hard for her and her colleagues to know where to start. All of that must have been on Sofia's mind that day, when she suddenly said to me, "We're in a state of triage right now in our district. I wish we could focus on learning, rather than treatment."

At the time, I had never thought about the problem of instructional improvement in precisely this way. The best way to illustrate the idea of triage probably comes from the process of prioritizing medical patients in emergency situations when medical resources are limited. The word comes from the French verb *trier*— "to separate, sift, or select." In effect, Sofia was saying that she dreads making decisions about which educational emergency she should be working on next, rather than thinking about the future learning of everyone. Sofia's statement went to the heart of how she experiences her work as an educator, and it describes a major dilemma that she shares with educators across this country: how do we educators focus on (or reorganize for) learning when we're really organized for triage? This dilemma, and the very different work conditions it implies, casts a long shadow on Sofia's school system and across this country. Part of my agreement with Lakeside was to help it think through this dilemma along the way, a practice that should be useful for any school system interested in instructional improvement.

Therefore, the lessons from this account of instructional rounds can be extended to school systems across America currently experiencing a similar set of challenges. Most school systems in this country are operating under an external accountability system that requires them to triage their responses: they look for quick fixes and increases in test scores, or risk being subject to a set of increasingly punitive measures meant to push them into compliance. Most of these school systems are already working as hard as they can. All of them would like to be doing better than they are currently doing. Unfortunately, in the places where politicians and other leaders have pushed too hard too quickly, principals, teachers, and administrators have recently been found resorting to cheating to meet these short-term demands to increase standardized test scores. This is why it's so important for all of us to pay attention to how Lakeside manages these pressures as they use instructional rounds.

## THE PROCESS OF INSTRUCTIONAL ROUNDS

Although we will look at the instructional rounds process in detail in Part I of this book, a few points here can serve as a foundation for readers less familiar with the practice. In particular, there are some important differences between instructional rounds and other ways of doing classroom observations in schools, since classroom observations are at the core of the practice. I'll say more about these differences later in the book, but they are critical to an understanding of how difficult some of the work was for Lakeside.

Most of the U.S. school districts that are practicing instructional rounds are using a process explained in a book by Elizabeth City, Richard Elmore, Sarah Fiarman, and Lee Teitel: *Instructional Rounds in Education: A Network Approach to Improving Teaching and Learning*. The authors describe instructional rounds as a process that "sits at the intersection of three current popular approaches to improvement . . . walkthroughs, networks, and district improvement strategies." Each of these three approaches has played a role in most educators' professional lives in separate ways, but City and her colleagues have integrated them into a set of protocols and a process that requires sustained attention to classroom observation in service of a widely shared problem of practice. A *problem of practice* is a statement that describes the instructional problem that a school is struggling with and that serves as a focus for classroom observations. The rounds process begins when the network (that's how City el al. refer to the people who practice rounds together) identifies a problem of practice it wants to focus on during the classroom observations. For example, the problems of practice in Lakeside will often sound something like this: *Many students are able to answer simple problems, but when they are asked to answer deep or multistep problems (such as those found in open-response exam items), they frequently shut down or give up. Many will stop reading/writing/thinking the moment they encounter a task that gives them difficulty.*

Networks can be created in a variety of ways, but in Lakeside's case, the network comprises all thirty-eight high school principals and the district office staff that supports the high schools. One of the principals agrees to host the network at his or her school and tailors the problem of practice to the specific context and needs of the school. Three or four of the other principals agree to visit the host principal's school and bring several teacher-leaders with them on the day of the school visit. Three or four teacher-leaders from the host school also participate in the classroom observations. The group of educators divides into subgroups of four and visits four or five classrooms for twenty minutes each.

Right away, it's easy to recognize how this process is a little different from other classroom observation processes with which many educators are familiar—the network focuses its observations on what the host school wants the observers to pay attention to, not what the outsiders think they should be doing. In addition, none of the observers will use a predetermined observation protocol or checklist during the observations. Rather, each observer will take detailed, descriptive notes about what he or she sees and hears in the classroom—observations related to the host school's problem of practice. This practice of observing lays a foundation for a discussion that is grounded in evidence, rather than any person's assumptions about what should or should not be happening in classrooms. Instructional rounds also differs in important ways from coaching models that are meant to improve classroom instruction—those models are usually about repeated one-on-one interactions between teachers and a coach or coaches. The idea behind this is that the coaches can identify the individual needs of the teacher and observe the teacher after targeted professional development around specific needs. In contrast, instructional rounds is always practiced in teams and focuses on broad patterns of instruction across schools, rather than the practice, or problems of practice, of individual teachers.

After several hours of classroom observations in four or five classrooms, each group will return to a predetermined room for a debrief of the evidence that the teams have collected in relation to the problem of practice. Each individual contributes a set of six to ten observations to his or her team's body of evidence, and each group will contribute a set of patterns that the whole group will discuss. In Sofia's case, she asks each individual to write his or her observations on yellow sticky notes and to place these on a flip chart next to the sticky notes of the other group members. Each individual then reads his or her sticky notes aloud, while the other group members make sure the observations don't contain any judgments or assumptions about the teaching or teacher.

Over the next few hours, the group will be required to look for patterns in the data that help to describe the teaching and learning that is happening *across classrooms in the school* and related to the problem of practice. Again, this process is distinct from many other classroom walkthrough processes, where the visiting team often spends just five or ten minutes in each classroom and leaves the school without discussing the observations with each other or with other educators in the school. In addition, in the instructional rounds process at Lakeside, there is almost no discussion of individual teachers; rather, the unit of analysis here is the school and the *system*, and the system's interest in a generating a common definition of rigorous instruction and rigorous classroom tasks. The theory behind this focus on broad patterns is that it gives the system more potential leverage than a series of teacher-specific, individual interventions with teachers.

During the last hour or two of the network's day-long rounds visit, Sofia asks each group to make some predictions about what students are learning in the school, according to the patterns and other evidence gathered during the classroom observations. This predictive stance helps the school and network decide whether there is a relationship between instructional practice and the problem of practice the host has been working on. In many cases, these predictions reveal important relationships between what students are being asked to do, and their performance across the school. But the predictions can also reveal new iterations and revisions of the problem of practice. In other words, practicing rounds regularly is really a way for the school system to engage in serial problem solving of an instructional problem—as the observers gather data related to that problem, the statement gets revised and refined to better reflect what educators are learning about instruction.

During the last half hour or so, the entire group will provide the host school with a set of recommendations that are based on the discussion of the data. In particular, the network will try to answer these questions: What should the school do or learn next? What should the observers do or learn next? These questions activate one last important distinction between rounds and other classroom walk-through programs: instructional rounds is ultimately about the ongoing learning of the adults doing the observations, and adult learning is a precursor to any learning expected of students.

During my first conversation with Sofia, she explained the interest in learning and Lakeside's hopes for instructional rounds, more generally:

> I go to all of these meetings, and everybody is in triage: "We need more assessments. I need the scores to go up." I think the leaders and the principals—there's a lot of pressure for them to improve test scores. That's how you get measured, and you could lose your job. So, there's a lot of pressure there. But hopefully, we'll move to a model that's more a healthy lifestyle versus constantly trying to fix a deficit in children. If we all behave in a healthy way and are building instructional rounds, if we engage in healthy behaviors, then maybe we won't have to be so triaged.

Sofia's supervisors made a huge investment of time and resources toward instructional rounds. In particular, Karen, one of the academic superintendents, was an early supporter of rounds, and Sofia wanted me to understand Karen's commitment to changing the culture of the system. I asked her to explain what a healthy lifestyle might look like in the schools:

If your doctor tells you that you need to sleep more, eat better, and exercise more, that would be a lifestyle change. Lots of individuals with unhealthy lifestyles continuously go to the doctor for acute medical problems. They are in a cycle of treatment. While it's difficult to pinpoint the exact benefits of a healthy lifestyle change to any one particular change in behavior, we know they happen over time and that the overall effect is beneficial. As you change your lifestyle, eventually the lifestyle will reduce the need for discrete medical treatment.

For a school system to have a healthy lifestyle, there needs to be structures in place for teachers to talk about problems of practice, discuss strategies for improvement, observe and analyze each other's practice, and set goals for the next level of work. I think one way to create the environment for schools to change their lifestyle is through this process of conducting instructional rounds. The current state of our schools is triage. We look at data to measure deficits and then figure out what to do to remediate these deficits . . . Perhaps, if we change our lifestyle, this triage effect will decrease and we will be able to focus more on learning, rather than treatment.

Lakeside's wish to focus on learning seems simple, but the reasons why Sofia and her colleagues have difficulty doing this are many. A state of triage is a poor environment for learning, but it's also a completely rational response, given the way most large school systems like Lakeside are typically organized, and given the history of schooling in America more generally. This history is one of long-standing traditions of autonomy of individual classrooms and schools.[3] In contrast, rounds would require educators to open up classrooms and schools to sustained observation in the interest of the learning of teams, a network, and of the system.[4] Perhaps most important, rounds would require the principals and other leaders in the system to *behave like learners*, rather than supervisors, and to model the kinds of learning they hope other educators and students might do. It was this learning stance, perhaps more than anything else, that would take the longest for everyone in the district to grasp.

Besides trying to adopt this learning stance for adults—and violating numerous cultural norms of privacy and autonomy of schools and school systems along the way—the practice of instructional rounds also pushes up against two other features of schooling that make this work difficult. First, instructional rounds tends to conflict with some of the more common structural arrangements of schooling that make working in teams and large networks quite difficult. In particular, like nearly all school districts in this country, Lakeside had a largely bureaucratic, hierarchical arrangement that was in conflict with the flat, mostly role-neutral arrangement that the instructional rounds network would require. Second, the work of instructional rounds happens on top of layer upon layer of other school reform efforts in places like Lakeside. As a result, teachers and other educators have good reason to be skeptical that instructional rounds might offer them something better than or different from the other reforms they have already endured. Therefore, these various challenges—a culture of privacy, hierarchies of school systems, and the history of school reform more generally—are important considerations for instructional rounds.

In the meantime, Lakeside's interest in focusing on the learning of adults will continue to complete with a host of other issues that pull the district in a hundred directions at once, each one signaling a different requirement or idea about how schools are supposed to improve. In the three years since Sofia and I had that first conversation, we have studied her district's effort to introduce this adult learning process throughout the system, often under conditions that don't necessarily give her or her colleagues any signals or incentives to focus on the learning of adults. This book attempts to explain how Sofia's team tried to stay focused on learning under these conditions. Understanding this effort is an essential step toward improving school systems, regardless of whether one thinks that instructional rounds is the way forward, and will help explain in practical terms why large-scale instructional improvement remains so persistently difficult.

## INSTRUCTIONAL ROUNDS AND LAKESIDE'S GOALS

As we will see, Lakeside has to constantly answer questions from teachers and principals about the purpose and practice of instructional rounds and its relationship to the district's broader improvement goals. Rounds was meant to support these goals, the most important of which the superintendent formally expressed in this way: "Today, [we offer] the best education possible for *some* of our students. [We] have the capacity to offer the best education possible for *all* of our students." To meet this goal, Lakeside also intends to "ensure all students achieve proficiency," "close access and achievement gaps," and "graduate all students from high school prepared for college completion and career success."

These goals seem relatively straight forward. The leadership wants to meet the state's Adequate Yearly Progress targets, close "achievement gaps," and crack the notoriously difficult case of improving high schools. These have been mostly intractable, ongoing problems for the district—the problems of this district are the problems of large school districts across the United States, to one degree or another. Despite huge investments of time and resources and the best intentions of educators across the district, these goals have thus far been mostly immune to a series of reform efforts. Indeed, in a recent system-wide curriculum audit, the district identified over three hundred distinct instructional programs and interventions, which run the gamut from workshop-style reading and writing, to restorative justice programs, to connected math programs. But the difference in test scores between white students and black and Latino students in this district is large and persistent.

However, rounds didn't offer the district any readily identifiable solutions, curriculum, or programs to implement in the classroom. This particular improvement effort was remarkable both for its intended scope in a sector accustomed to isolated success and for the complexity of the learning required of the adults doing the work. That this effort required people to do things they did not know how to do and had never done before is no small matter. That the learning of each individual and school was partly dependent on the learning of other individuals and schools marks a substantive, critical shift in the district's school improvement plan.

## THE PROBLEMS OF ORGANIZATIONAL LEARNING

A complete account of instructional rounds in Lakeside Public Schools is far too large and complex to analyze completely in this book. The story is partly about the complex relationship between educators' practice, their students, and a lot of curricular content and the impact the process might ultimately have on the learning of students.[5] However, the main focus of this book is *how* and *why* this school system uses rounds, what the educators think they are learning as a result, and whether their efforts can tell us anything useful about the problems of implementing large-scale instructional improvement.

As I have already suggested, beginning an improvement process of this magnitude and level of conviction will surface a number of problems within the organization. Most school systems have some capacity for supporting teaching and learning, but few have any experience with supporting a dramatic and widespread shift in the relationship between the district office and schools, let alone the new problems that arise when educators systematically spend time in one another's classrooms and schools. Some of these new problems are a good thing: most educators now accept the idea that schools need to pay more attention to their core business of learning and teaching, and rounds initially give people an excuse to test-drive a model for doing just that. But as we'll see, this district has much less experience identifying and dealing with the subsequent organizational problems that get activated when it practices rounds weekly, expects rounds to improve teaching and learning, or tries to connect rounds to a broader plan for instructional improvement.

My focus on these organizational problems also reveals an important bias to this book: like the authors of *Instructional Rounds*, I believe that what distinguishes instructional rounds from virtually all other school improvement ideas is that it is intended to disrupt the typical patterns of interaction between adults in schools. Disrupting these patterns activates organizational problems that few school systems have any experience in solving—problems that ultimately have to be solved if they are to improve. Although we'll return to this idea of problematizing organizational learning, the reader should be aware from the beginning that I view the rounds process through this lens. In the next sections, I provide an initial description of what four of these organizational problems look like in Lakeside Public Schools.

## The Problem of Frequency

Imagine a medical profession where new surgeons practice once or twice alone before performing their first solo surgery. Or an engineering firm where the structural engineers don't talk to the architects, who in turn only speak to the materials scientists after the bridge is built. Or a professional soccer team that only holds practice on the chalkboard, instead of the soccer pitch, and typically only once or twice a year. Can you imagine boarding a plane where the pilot and crew have under their belt only a couple of spins together in a simulator?

These ideas are completely nonsensical in their respective fields, but it is exactly the conditions that the Lakeside school system regularly finds itself when it tries to use instructional rounds to improve teaching and learning. Most school districts—with the best of intentions—are asking educators to do highly technical, high-stakes work in the classroom with very little time or space for practice, team work, or simulations of the kind of work that they think might be successful. In fact, educators report that the professional development they receive often takes place away from the classroom and separate from their colleagues. Much like the soccer team that holds practice on the chalkboard—this approach might be good in theory, but the real work is much more fluid and complicated when implemented on the field. Indeed, finding a way to structure teachers' workdays so that they can practice in teams every week is an important technical challenge that the Lakeside network will need to solve.

The first problem this school system confronted when it implemented instructional rounds is precisely this technical problem: how to make time and space for educators to *regularly* learn together in groups. I'll refer to this as the *problem of frequency*. Unfortunately, most educators initially experience rounds as an *event*, rather than as a regular, ongoing improvement practice. To put it bluntly, educators who practice rounds a couple of times a year are probably not improving their practice. Put another way, the system should not expect anything of the process if educators "do rounds" a couple of times a year. As we'll later see, the Lakeside schools that have solved the problem of frequency are learning a great deal more about the organization and are better positioned to learn something from the rounds practice.

### The Problem of Symmetry

Educators in Sofia's school system regularly express a desire to see their students complete more rigorous school work. By *rigorous*, they typically mean school tasks where students are able to have conversations with one another, using academic language, and produce individual or group products that show command of the academic language and an understanding of how different concepts relate to one another. Some of the teachers I spoke with say they know how to design these kinds of lessons. Some of them say they actually do assign these kinds of lessons regularly. But all of them had personal theories on why this kind of work does not (or cannot) happen more regularly in high schools.

In every way, the rounds process is *exactly* the kind of rigorous task that many educators wish their students were able to do more frequently. It is a cognitively demanding group process that requires high levels of sustained effort and an understanding of how different instructional concepts might be related to one another. Educators regularly practicing rounds have to analyze observation data, predict what the students might be learning, and defend their own ideas to feel that they are having success during the process. However, many Lakeside teachers initially dislike rounds for the very reasons that make it a rigorous task: some of the work is ambiguous, and it is often emotionally challenging.

The problem of symmetry is both a technical and a cultural problem that this district had to confront: how will the learning we do as adults model the type of learning that we expect of students? When organizational learning is symmetric, educators are engaging in the same kinds of learning that they expect of students. Further, every adult in the system should have the same basic requirements for learning, regardless of his or her role or position in the system.

## The Problem of Reciprocity

I've attended instructional rounds at most of the high schools in this district. In every case, these visits were attended by several teachers and principals from other high schools in the district—they are there to participate, learn, and be part of offering feedback to the host school. These visiting educators regularly report that the visit helped them adapt the rounds process for *their* school and that the observation data from the visit is informing *their* professional development for instructional improvement. However, these educators often report in the same breath that they do not really see the point in having to do rounds in schools that are not their own.

Thus, the *problem of reciprocity* is largely a cultural problem: How will we help each other learn within this system of learning we've created? And how will we know if people are doing anything with that learning? When educators in a school system are asked (and sometimes required) to help each other learn, the organization is pushing a countercultural practice that is much more nuanced than previous conceptions of evaluation and supervision.[6] Reciprocal learning is also contrary to the assumptions of the current school-level accountability system. Under such a system, educators often believe the schools are being measured against one another, which makes this problem all the more persistent and pernicious.

## The Problem of (Not) Talking About Race

Despite the complications of these organizational problems, the most difficult question that Lakeside faces has to do with the achievement gaps that persist in the district. Educators have very different explanations and understandings of these racial differences, and this affects how they process classroom observation data during instructional rounds. In particular, we'll think about the following questions: How does rounds support or limit the ways that educators deal with racial differences in the student body? What happens when educators disagree about—or aren't able to discuss—race and racial patterns during rounds? And what might these conversations reveal about how a system might better manage these topics during instructional rounds? Lakeside has widely publicized throughout the community that one of the goals of the school system is to close the achievement gaps between white students and students of color in the district. Nevertheless, conversations about race during instructional rounds, or following classroom observations, are virtually nonexistent. When they do occur, they typically end as quickly as they begin, suggesting that instructional rounds doesn't provide educators with the common language or support to deal with these topics in groups of their colleagues.

Some readers may wonder whether it is helpful to view race through the lens of instructional rounds, because their assumption is that the rounds process is necessarily color-blind. Indeed, those who are primarily interested in the technical details of rounds and protocol will no doubt argue that rounds should be studied completely separate from contextual factors like race. My own view is that any question we ask about school improvement—and rounds—should take into account educators' understanding of race and their explanations for differences in student performance. In any event, understanding these racial differences is important to Sofia and to her school system, and so we will deal with it directly in this book.

## HOW TO READ THIS BOOK

My intent is to use this example of instructional rounds practiced widely in Lakeside Public Schools to illustrate some of the practical problems that arise in large-scale instructional improvement, and some potential solutions to those problems. In fact, a great deal of evidence suggests that school systems everywhere share these problems. Indeed, if large-scale instructional improvement seems to fail almost everywhere in the United States, there must be some common problems across these systems. If there are common problems, then there are also common solutions.

This book also focuses primarily on the learning of adults and the organization writ large, while acknowledging the lack of formal research on the impact of instructional rounds on student learning. Despite these important unanswered questions, it is nevertheless important to understand *how* adults learn, despite the real problems revealed by educators' participation in instructional rounds.

Educators regularly engaged in this rounds work are also starting to ask sophisticated questions about the rounds practice and its relationship to other improvement processes with which they are familiar. Anecdotal reports about the process in schools through district- and state-funded programs detail high levels of satisfaction and a promising professional mechanism. However, these cases also show that definitions of instructional rounds practices vary across organizational contexts and school settings. Part of my motive for investigating rounds is to begin to clarify some of these differences, not to measure whether rounds "works." By understanding what happened in the Lakeside district, we might better understand how to undertake large-scale instructional improvement.

There are also some strengths to my approach. Unlike typical case studies, which are often based solely on the retrospective of participants, I was present for approximately 150 hours of rounds in twenty high schools during the academic year. This level of participation allows me to give a detailed account of the process as it happened, without having to rely solely on the memory or perceptions of educators.

I came to this research about instructional rounds as a former teacher, principal, and doctoral student interested in classroom instruction. Richard Elmore initially drew me into the practice by inviting me along with him as he facilitated the rounds process in various settings. I subsequently learned the practice alongside Liz City, Sarah Fiarman, Lee Teitel, Stefanie Reinhorn, and Tim O'Brien as we helped to build networks of educators learning and using the practice, and developed the Instructional Rounds Institute at the Harvard Graduate School of Education.

While I was learning alongside these people, I also started a school-based rounds network at a charter high school. The network began with a small group of teachers in the school and grew to include every teacher in the school practicing rounds once per week. This book, in other words, is shaped heavily by my experience of working with practitioners as they learned and adapted the practice to a variety of school settings.

In the chapters that follow, I report patterns in my observation and interview data, but ground those findings in specific ideas about what we might learn about rounds and large-scale improvement more generally. In trying to be conscious of the different assumptions and entry points of the reader, I asked a set of questions meant to help readers understand the participants' experiences and their understanding of the district's improvement process. Broadly speaking, the questions are as follows:

- What do educators actually do when they say they are doing rounds?
- Why do they think they are practicing instructional rounds?
- What do they think they're learning through this process?
- How do they understand race and racial differences during the process?
- In light of the data, what could we reasonably expect the organization to learn in the long term, if this work were to continue?

Rounds is an adult learning process usually practiced under accountability conditions that don't always allow or make time for the process, in organizations that don't necessarily know how to support adult learning. Thus, we can rewrite Sofia's dilemma into the following questions about systemic school improvement that will serve as the basis for this book: What kinds of broad organizational problems get activated during instructional rounds? How does a system reorganize to manage those problems under conditions that previously made triage, rather than learning, a rational choice?

## OVERVIEW OF THE BOOK

The book is divided into three sections that will take us progressively deeper into the district's experience with the rounds process. Part 1, "Organizing for Instructional Rounds," explores the impact of practicing rounds regularly and widely across a system. We'll see how the Lakeside school district initially organized to practice instructional rounds in every high school, and some of the reasons why educators think they are doing this work. As we'll see, the answer to *why* isn't initially as clear-cut as we might want, but it does help to explain the difficulties of generating a common vision for improvement. Chapters 1 and 2 provide some background on the district and a mostly descriptive account of a typical rounds day. Chapter 3 describes the district's theory of action and establishes the system-level rationale and current ideas about how the district intends to improve. The chapter compares these ideas with what some individual educators think they are supposed to be learning or doing with the rounds process. Chapter 4 gives an extended account of the instructional problems the schools think they are supposed to be solving through the rounds process. The goal of this chapter is to analyze an emerging tension between locating instructional problems in the student body, and locating them in teachers' practice.

Part 2, "Solving Problems of Organizational Learning," is devoted to Sofia's dilemma—about the specific problems a school system has to manage during the transition away from triage and more toward adult learning. We'll look at three systemic problems of adult learning: frequency, symmetry, reciprocity. These examples reveal patterns in the beliefs and actions of adults practicing instructional rounds. I'll describe the solutions that the school system has initially applied to these problems, and offer some lessons learned from these efforts.

In Part 3, "Future Challenges," I describe some ongoing problems for the school system—problems for which the system currently has no broad solutions. In Chapters 8, I explore how educators process race and racial differences in the student body during instructional rounds. This analysis should help describe why discussing race and achievement gaps during instructional rounds remains so persistently difficult. Chapter 9 summarizes the lessons learned from the entire book and suggests some ongoing dilemmas and questions.

Finally, in our work with school systems, my colleagues and I often use a protocol called "Save the Last Word," from the National School Reform Faculty. The purpose of this protocol is to help educators clarify and deepen their thinking about a text they read together. The protocol allows each person in a group a turn to talk, while giving the "last word" to the person who agreed to share his or her thinking first. In that spirit, I've offered Lakeside the last word of this book. In her afterword, "Does Rounds Work? The View from Lakeside," Sofia responds to the question that many educators ask about rounds, and she talks about the changes she has seen in Lakeside over the past three years.

# PART 1

# Organizing for Instructional Rounds

"The ongoing improvement of both student learning and instructional practices is the primary focus of the superintendent's agenda. As schools are charged to organize and work to attain these goals, it becomes contingent upon the district offices to provide support in this endeavor. To this end, this office will continue to join all high schools in the implementation of instructional rounds. The purpose of rounds is to deepen the knowledge and skills of the group and to provide helpful feedback and suggestions of support for the host school. Discussion is geared around the central belief that improvement can occur through changes in the relationship of students and teachers in the presence of content.

The rounds process consists of an orientation meeting with the headmaster and team; observation of practice; observation debrief; next level of work analysis; and an optional after-school meeting with faculty. The process is about creating and modeling a specific set of ideas about how schools and systems can learn from their own practices, developing an understanding of the next problem they need to solve, and taking control of their own learning in ways that are more likely to lead to sustained improvement over time."

*—Lakeside Public Schools Central Office*
*introductory letter to high school principals*

## CHAPTER 1

# A System in Transition

## From "Learning Walks" to Instructional Rounds

I think it was hard for me to change, first. I had been part
of a culture where we did walk-throughs and we did learning walks
and all these criteria-based observations and thinking about what
was missing [in the classroom]. When I first experienced rounds,
I was kind of angry. I simmered on that. I thought about it for a long time,
and I realized this needs to be the work. Instructional rounds needs
to be the work. So I thought, "How am I going to make this my work?"

—*Sofia, Lakeside Public Schools' instructional rounds facilitator*

In 2009, the Lakeside high schools adopted a system-wide instructional focus on something they call "rigor."[1] The principals of the high schools meet on a monthly basis for professional development to talk about both instructional and operational issues, and their conversations about rigor began during those meetings. Their initial ideas grew out of a practice of watching classroom videos together as part of their professional development. When they first tried to analyze these videos together, they rarely agreed on what they thought instruction should look like—in particular, they disagreed on what teachers and students actually do in rigorous classrooms. For example, one of their typical activities was to rate the rigor in a classroom, on a scale from 1 (lowest) to 5 (highest) after watching each video. In nearly every case, there were as many principals who would rate a classroom a 1 as who would rate the same classroom a 5.

It became clear to Sofia, Karen (the academic superintendent for high schools), and many of the principals that there was little agreement about what rigor was or how the administrators and principals would support or supervise teachers in their efforts toward rigorous instruction. Although the high school principals developed a working document for what they thought rigor should look like in the classroom (figure 1.1), this only captured the huge range of ideas that existed in the system. No one who was involved with its development was satisfied with this rigor document or with what it said about the role of students and teachers in the instructional process.[2] But it was a start, and it provides some background for what educators were working on and thinking about when they first considered using instructional rounds.

At the time, Sofia, Karen, and their colleagues in the district office had no unifying approach to the principals' various views on rigor. The program they *did* have—"learning walks"—was built for an entirely different purpose than that of instructional rounds. Sofia had been a regular participant in learning walks both as a teacher and as an administrator. As a teacher, Sofia recalled how her principal described the program: "He called it the dog and pony show. We put on our best clothes, pull out our best lesson, and everything goes back to normal after it's over."

Later, as an administrator, Sofia and her colleagues in the central office would visit each high school once during the school year. The group would walk the halls with the principal and perhaps an assistant principal or instructional leader from the school. They would observe five to ten classrooms, usually for no more than ten minutes each. As Sofia suggested above, these learning walks were based on a set of criteria developed by the district office, but the criteria were largely unknown to the instructional staff of the high schools. Sofia and her colleagues were looking for rigor, but didn't necessarily agree on what it should look like. In any event, the purpose of the learning walks was to help the principals and schools improve instruction, but it wasn't clear how the act of observing the teachers would translate into more teacher knowledge about rigor and, subsequently, better instruction. At the end of the classroom observations, Sofia and her associates would leave the school, often without talking with the other educators about what they saw. Most educators simply complied with the visit once a year and then went back to doing what they already knew how to do.

While learning walks can take a variety of forms in American schools—some are about learning and improvement; others are cursory and punitive—many educators believe that this approach doesn't give them much traction with the problems that are important to them and certainly not a common definition of rigorous

---

**FIGURE 1.1**

## Defining academic rigor

| High expectations + | High relevance + | Appropriate support = | Higher student engagement and learning |
|---|---|---|---|
| Teacher utilizes content objectives aligned with common local, state, or external standards. | Teacher builds on students' prior knowledge (cultural, personal, etc.) to introduce new concepts. | Teacher and students cultivate positive relationships with one another in order to enhance learning. | Students actively and responsibly participate in the learning process. They know what's expected of them. |
| Teacher engages students in active reasoning and critical thinking (upper levels of Bloom's [Taxonomy of Educational Objectives]) —questions and assigned tasks. | Teacher presents concepts in multiple forms (i.e., graphs, numerical, words). | Teacher gradually releases responsibility to students. | Students raise questions, solve problems, analyze, apply, synthesize, evaluate, and/or create. |
| Teacher ensures accountable student talk and writing. | Teacher utilizes differentiated instructional practices. | Teacher uses word walls, graphic organizers, and technology in the classroom to support students. | Students engage with classmates regarding the content. |
| Teacher acts as "guide on the side, not sage on the stage." | Teacher utilizes a variety of assessments to inform daily instruction. | Teacher individualizes support based on student needs. | Students complete rigorous, relevant, high-level assignments. They understand their own learning styles. |

*Lakeside Public Schools' working definitions for rigor, developed jointly with the high school principals.*

---

instruction. But in the year after they first began focusing on rigor, Sofia and her colleagues continued with the learning-walks approach because they didn't have another way of getting into schools and classrooms to observe instruction. It wasn't until the end of their first year focusing on rigor that Sofia learned another way to do that work. She spent a couple of days as a participant of instructional rounds in a nearby school district, learning the protocols and the purpose for the practice. As she described in the beginning of this chapter, the experience was not at all pleasant for her. For this reason, a suitable starting point for describing what happened in Lakeside is to explain why instructional rounds might initially make Sofia, or any educator, angry. This explanation will tell us a little bit about the Lakeside school district and a lot about instructional rounds. It also will help to illustrate an issue that will recur throughout this chapter and the next: rounds initially makes educators quite uncomfortable, but this discomfort seems to be an important precursor to productive conversations about teaching and learning.

There are a number of ways in which rounds initially made Sofia angry, but for our purposes in this book, two will initially suffice here. First, rounds brought into sharp relief for her the inconsistencies and inefficiencies of the learning walks she had been doing for many years. Although the walk-throughs were meant to help the schools, she realized that the schools had no theory or process for how the information was supposed to pass from the observers to the many teachers in the schools, and this was a hard realization for an educator like Sofia to come to terms with. In contrast, when she participated in instructional rounds, Sofia observed and debriefed *with* teams of teachers and principals who would be ultimately responsible for that instruction. This ensured that Sofia and the educators with whom she observed were at least starting to develop some common language about what they were seeing in classrooms. The second way that instructional rounds initially upset her is that it required her to act like a learner, rather than a supervisor. Although Sofia is very open to learning and feedback, even she admits that it was difficult to adopt that learning stance in groups of educators who also weren't always accustomed to thinking of themselves as learners. Taken together, these two facts make it understandable that an educator like Sofia would leave her first experience with instructional rounds feeling confused and perhaps even angry about the way she had spent the past few years working in Lakeside.

Importantly, Sofia isn't unusual in feeling this way. This sentiment, or something like it, gets expressed regularly by educators who experience rounds for the first time in Lakeside and elsewhere. Many report feeling very disoriented by the process, particularly those observing classroom instruction for the first time in many years. Others enjoy the observations, but find working in teams with their colleagues to be terribly frustrating. Still others have trouble understanding how instructional rounds compare with other classroom observation experiences they have had, particularly learning walks. Nearly all of the participants in instructional rounds say that they learned something about their role as an educator, but not all of them want to do it again. This chapter and the next describe why this might be and what educators can learn about instruction—and one another—along the way.

## PREPPING PEOPLE FOR ROUNDS

After stewing over their initial experience with instructional rounds for part of the summer, Karen decided to shift from learning walks to instructional rounds and appointed Sofia to lead that effort. As their above-quoted introductory letter to the principals suggests, instructional rounds is not something a system can do well without some preparation. To begin, the district spent the summer disseminating information through formal, written channels and at the high school principals' professional development meetings. All thirty-eight high school principals were assigned common reading about instructional rounds. Together with the Lakeside Public Schools Central Office, the principals then spent the early fall watching videos of classroom instruction from a variety of sources outside their own school district and debriefing their observations using the instructional rounds protocols (figure 1.2).

---

### FIGURE 1.2

#### THE INSTRUCTIONAL ROUNDS PROCESS

1. **Observe.** Take notes on what you see and hear related to the host school's problem of practice.

2. **Describe.** In teams, describe what you saw, using specific, nonjudgmental language.

3. **Analyze.** Look for patterns across classrooms, giving names to categories and patterns.

4. **Predict.** In light of your group's evidence, predict what students are learning.

5. **Next level of work.** What should the school do or learn next? What should the observers do or learn next?

---

*Source:* Adapted from Elizabeth A. City, Richard F. Elmore, Sarah E. Fiarman, and Lee Teitel, *Instructional Rounds in Education: A Network Approach to Improving Teaching and Learning* (Cambridge, MA: Harvard Education Press, 2009).

There are a couple of reasons why the district spent this much time prepping the principals. First, as Sofia learned the hard way, practicing instructional rounds is fundamentally different from the school review programs the district has used in the past. In other words, instructional rounds requires a completely different skill set of both principals and district office staff. In particular, the instructional rounds network the district was planning required principals to visit classrooms in schools that were not their own and to spend time debriefing what they saw in teams with teachers and Lakeside staff.[3] Karen and Sofia began with the principals and central office staff, considering this the best group to start generating some common ideas around rigor.

At the same time that the district was prepping principals, it was also planning to include instructional staff in the rounds process. In a system of many thousands of teachers, it was not feasible for Lakeside to train each teacher. Instead, Sofia explained that the district wanted to "seed" instructional rounds in each high school. The expectation was that as principals learned the process by visiting other schools, they would involve their own instructional staff over time. All of this meant that the principals would be training a lot of educators in the moment, during the actual school visit. The purpose of many of the early rounds visits would be to help principals, teachers, and district staff learn the instructional rounds protocols. Nevertheless, one fact stands out in this plan: every high school in the district would participate, and all thirty-eight schools would be visited in one academic year. One can imagine any number of other, more conservative schedules that Lakeside might have tried, but the district office was clear on this point: it wanted the entire system of high schools working together to learn and use rounds.

After several months of preparation, Sofia organized the thirty-eight principals for school visits (figure 1.3). Each principal was scheduled to visit two other schools for rounds during the academic year, and each was scheduled to host one school visit at his or her own school. While Sofia and her colleagues in the central office left it up to the principals to decide which teachers to invite on the classroom observations with them, the expectation was that the principals would involve instructional staff. Sofia would facilitate all of the network visits, and Karen and other district staff would rotate their attendance and participation. In theory, this network design meant that each principal would practice three times during the year with two other principals who were part of the small group, in addition to some instructional staff. In total, thirty-eight high schools in the system would be visited, averaging about two per week from late October through late May.

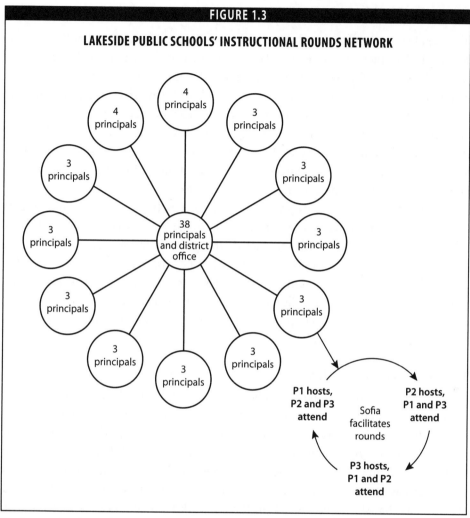

**FIGURE 1.3**

**LAKESIDE PUBLIC SCHOOLS' INSTRUCTIONAL ROUNDS NETWORK**

*The instructional rounds network consists of thirty-eight high school principals (labeled P1, P2, etc., on right side of figure) and the district office members that support high schools in Lakeside. Sofia (the instructional rounds facilitator for the high schools) would facilitate each day of rounds (on average, two times per week, although rounds happens less frequently during mandatory testing periods). The academic superintendent and other district staff would rotate their participation on rounds each week. Typically, several teachers would conduct the observations with the principals on each rounds day. Some of these teachers were educators in the host school, and the visiting principals would typically bring three or four teachers along so that the rounds group consisted of twelve to fifteen observers in total.*

## A PICTURE OF ROUNDS

The next few sections of this chapter will provide a detailed account of how educators typically practice rounds in Lakeside. While this description will focus heavily on the steps Sofia uses to lead a group of educators through the process, we'll also look at some of the moments of clarity and confusion that typically arise. The detailed description of the rounds process may feel strange to some readers: few studies of school improvement efforts dedicate this much space to describing in detail *how* educators actually do the work of interest. However, this description will be important for understanding the organizational problems we'll look at in subsequent chapters, where we'll return to these examples.

Like Sofia, many educators who experience instructional rounds come to realize that they don't often share common language about instruction and don't necessarily enjoy dealing with that fact in groups of their colleagues. In addition, taking on the characteristics of a learner is not necessarily an easy transition for educators, who are used to being teachers or supervisors, and it takes lots of repetition and practice with a skilled facilitator for most people to adopt that learning stance. These patterns will provide the foundation for discussing instructional rounds throughout this book.

### The Morning Rounds Meeting

It's mid-October in the Lakeside school district, and schools, teachers, and students are starting to settle into routines. On this particular morning, Jefferson High School will be operating outside those routines as a host of the instructional rounds network. Over the past few weeks, Sofia has met with Jefferson's principal and the instructional leadership team to develop and decide on a problem of practice. They have traded drafts of this statement, and Sofia has offered feedback and suggestions that she thinks will help the network focus its observations and the subsequent discussion on something observable in the classroom and related to the district's interest in rigor.

At a table in a conference room sit four teachers and the school's assistant principal. On the table is a stack of yellow folders. Sofia is untangling a nest of computer cords with one hand and holding a large cup of coffee with the other. The people at the table are each sitting quietly, and one of the teachers has opened her yellow folder and is reading a bright green piece of paper titled "Problem of Practice."

"We're just waiting on a few more people," Sofia says. "Dave called and said they would be a few minutes late. Traffic was pretty bad this morning, I guess." Dave is the science department head at Emerson High, across the city. He is bringing several other teachers and his principal with him this morning, which brings the total rounds group to fourteen people today—five visitors from Dave's school, five educators from the host school, and three members from Lakeside Public Schools Central Office, including Karen.

In the yellow folder are eight one-page documents:

1. Problem of Practice
2. School Profile
3. Agenda
4. District Theory of Action
5. Academic Rigor
6. Bloom's Taxonomy
7. Six Ways of Demonstrating Learning

The last document listed above is an adaptation of the performance levels from the Programme for International Assessment (PISA). The "Problem of Practice" and "School Profile" documents are written in a slightly different font than the other documents. This is because the host school's Instructional Leadership Team (ILT) has provided the problem of practice and school profile to help the group focus its observations in classrooms today—the other documents have been provided by Sofia and the district office. The group spends a few minutes reading the school's problem of practice:

### Problem of Practice

In the past, we have recognized that students arrive with low reading skills and stamina. Their underdeveloped strategies for reading and lack of confidence in approaching difficult texts lead to a minimal amount of reading outside of the classroom. The lack of outside reading requires teachers to utilize valuable instructional time highlighting main ideas and recalling basic plot details. With our growing population of English Language Learners, it is becoming more and more difficult to move beyond comprehension and into inference, analysis, and synthesis. Yet, it is the higher-order thinking that we ask students to demonstrate through critical reading and writing.

The variation of skills and motivation among students also requires teachers to design lessons to reach students with a wide range of abilities.

Our theory of action has been to provide professional development, department, grade-level, and student-support meetings, grading that is

consistent across the departments, and student supports (social, emotional, and academic). We also continually re-examine processes and utilize data to inform instruction.

Our improvement strategies include: active reading instruction, talking
to the text, small classes, learning centers for students who are struggling,
and differentiated instruction. We incorporate a variety of technologies
into daily lessons to engage and support student learning.

### Focus Questions
- How are teachers scaffolding instruction to prepare *all* students for
  higher-level critical thinking skills required for Honors, AP, and the SAT?
- How are *all* students responding to the content and current task?

By the time everyone finishes reading, Dave and his colleagues have arrived.
During the introductions that ensue, it is clear that none of the educators from
Emerson know any of the educators from Jefferson. This is not an unusual occurrence in Lakeside and part of the reason why the network requires these cross-
school visits. After a few minutes of introductions and conversation, Sofia looks
anxious to begin. She looks at her watch as she explains that the participants need
to be in classrooms by 8:25. "That gives us about forty-five minutes to talk about
why we're here, and look at the school's problem of practice," she says.

She walks the group through the agenda document, which outlines the sections
of rounds for the day. Sofia's plan is to spend the first few minutes talking about the
theory and purpose of instructional rounds. Then, she wants the participants to
practice using descriptive language in pairs with some image cards from a child's
game she has brought. Finally, she wants everyone to look at the school profile
and problem of practice before people organize into observations teams. After
four twenty-minute classroom observations, lunch will arrive, during which the
participants will start debriefing. Sofia expects that the group will finish its work
sometime just after 1:30 p.m. Her last statement gets Dave's attention.

"Sofia," he says, "just so you know, we need to leave by about 1:15 p.m. We have
a department meeting at 2 today."

"OK, no problem," she replies. "I'll see if I can push us a little faster during the
debrief, and we'll have a working lunch." Projected on the white, concrete block
wall at one end of the conference room is the following PowerPoint slide:

*Learning Goals:* Build Common Language. Develop skills to use descriptive, nonjudgmental language with a focus on the instructional core

for observing teaching and learning. Become familiar with the steps of rounds and the learning goals behind each step. Build capacity at the school site and view rounds as a process and not as a one-time event.

To understand this example of the rounds process, we need to understand all of the ways in which the goals on this simple PowerPoint slide contradict most educators' ideas about what their job is. In particular, the idea that the group needs to learn something today is hugely countercultural for several reasons. First, these educators have seldom been asked to learn something about instruction in a group of their colleagues, and it's countercultural because most mornings, these educators are probably thinking about what they should be teaching, not about what they should be learning. As I have explained elsewhere, a lot of school systems also don't have regularly recurring processes for this kind of adult group learning, and so the idea that the participants shouldn't view today "as a one-time event" is also probably hard to conceptualize for many of the educators in the room.

By the time Sofia finishes talking about the learning goals for the day, first period is just about to start beyond the walls of the conference room. This means there is plenty to distract the host staff members from the learning they are about to try. It's a new experience for them to be sitting here at this time of day and to block out everything happening in the hallways and classrooms. A few issues find their way into the room anyway—one of the school secretaries walks in to whisper something in the ear of the assistant principal, James, whose walkie-talkie has just squawked.

"Sorry," he says as he quickly turns it off. He whispers to the secretary, "No, I'm not sure if Mrs. Smith's sub has arrived. Do you mind handling it while I'm on the walkthrough? I mean, the rounds?" This kind of interaction is also not an unusual occurrence in the early months of rounds: the process requires sustained attention and a shift in educators' roles, and this adjustment takes a bit of time for everyone. Normally, James would be dealing with substitute teachers and parents—this morning, he'll be observing classrooms.

As the secretary shuts the door, Sofia advances the PowerPoint. The title of the next slide is "Group Norms." She reads three norms that she would like the group to adopt for today: "equity of voice," "active listening," and "respect for all perspectives."

"Can we also all agree that when I raise my hand, that's the quiet signal?" she asks. "That will be important later today, when we're working in groups." A few heads nod in agreement as she changes the slide again.

Sofia asks, "Dave, can you talk about this slide for the group? I know you've seen it a few times before on rounds and in our class."[4]

"Sure. No problem." Dave is sitting up straight in his chair now and takes a moment to read the slide (figure 1.4).

"This is the instructional core," he says. "I think of this as something that helps me figure out what to pay attention to when I'm observing in classrooms. Sometimes it gets a little hard to figure out what to pay attention to, especially when I'm in an English classroom or some other class where I don't know the subject matter. The whole idea of task is really important. It's the part in the center of the triangle. Kind of the intersection of the teacher and student with whatever they might be working on." A couple of heads nod in agreement. "How's that, Sofia?" Dave asks.

"That's perfect. Thanks, Dave," Sofia says.

---

## FIGURE 1.4

## The instructional core

**Theory**

- The instructional core: central belief that improvement can occur through changes in the relationship of students and teachers in the presence of content.

- Task predicts performance.

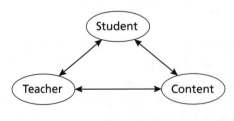

*Lakeside Public Schools' explanation and understanding of the instructional core.*

*Source:* The district adapted its explanation from Elizabeth A. City, Richard F. Elmore, Sarah E. Fiarman, and Lee Teitel, *Instructional Rounds in Education: A Network Approach to Improving Teaching and Learning* (Cambridge, MA: Harvard Education Press 2009).

As Dave suggests, a second challenge for many of the educators today will be deciding what to pay attention to when they observe in classrooms. The school's problem of practice and focus questions above will provide them with some guidance, but most educators who don't regularly observe in classrooms can find it a bit overwhelming. Sofia has provided them with another framework to help them with these observations, called the *instructional core*.[5]

In short, Sofia is asking them to block out everything except what they can actually observe students and teachers doing in the classroom. This is harder than it sounds, particularly because people naturally bring a set of assumptions about what they think *should* be happening in the classroom. Sofia wants the participants to set those things aside today and just record what they actually see or hear students and teachers doing with the content. If the observers do this well, she thinks the data will also help them make some predictions later about what they think students are learning today.

Sofia asks, "Do any other folks have any questions or want to say anything else about the instructional core? I think the most important part of this theory is that 'task predicts performance.' Kids will be able to do what we ask them to do on a regular basis. Can you all take out the blue sheet in your folder that says 'District Theory of Action' at the top? Let me know if anyone needs one, but it's also on the slide on the wall."

### Lakeside's Theory of Action

*If* the district *delivers* effective instruction that is both rigorous and relevant and *develops* the infrastructure necessary to increase the knowledge and skills to support and implement that instruction, *then* instructional practices will improve in *every school* and the quality of student work will increase. In addition, *if* every employee throughout the district (schools and central office) understands how his/her role impacts student performance and accepts *personal responsibility* for enabling all students to excel, *then* the achievement of students at all performance levels will accelerate, and we will close the achievement gap.

"This is the theory of action that was developed by the superintendent's office over the last couple of years," Sofia explains. "I'd like you all to spend a few minutes reading it and mark it up or write any questions or thoughts you might have. Then, we'll get into pairs and do a pair-share and hear from a couple of groups about what they came up with." The room immediately fills with chatter.

The underlying reason why this district practices rounds is still up for debate among many of the Lakeside administrators and educators, but figure 1.4, showing the district's theory of action, offers an entry point into understanding the rationale. First, the theory represents an attempt to articulate and share with educators the leadership's best ideas, at the moment, about the steps they think will lead to improvement. A second, more general point is that theories of action are increasingly used as part of school improvement efforts, and this one will provide an interesting case for readers to examine. Let's return to the discussion these educators are having about the theory of action.

An English teacher says to her partner, "I'm a little confused because this says 'If the district delivers effective instruction,' but the district doesn't really deliver instruction. The teachers do."

"I thought it meant that the district should support teachers and schools," remarks her partner. "I liked that part."

In another part of the room, James says, "I think the part about personal responsibility is really important. However, I think students have to have responsibility for their learning, and I don't see that part in here."

After about five minutes of conversation, Sofia raises her hand, and the room falls quiet.

"Does anyone want to share out what they talked about?"

"I will," says another English teacher. "I've never seen this theory of action before, but it was helpful to look at it. I think it's good that the district is talking about supporting teachers and also everyone understanding their role and how it impacts student performance. But there's a gap between theory and practice in the theory of action that we experience emotionally, and we need a team willing to have that conversation."

The idea that there might be a gap between what a large school system says it's doing and what educators are actually doing is not a new one, but looking at a theory of action tends to bring these gaps into sharper focus.

"Does anyone want to respond to her?" Sofia asks.

Dave raises his hand, and Sofia points to him.

"Well," he says, "I was just going to say that the part about infrastructure seems really important, but it could mean a couple of things. That could mean having buildings that have good science labs, but it could also mean professional development or giving teachers more time during school to plan lessons. Maybe they also mean that rounds is a kind of infrastructure, although I'm not sure."

James jumps in. "I think the most important thing is this part about all students excelling, not just some students. We need to bring up the bottom, but also keep pushing at the top, and I think that's the really hard part."

Clearly, these educators bring to the table different ideas about what Lakeside's theory of action means for them and about the kinds of actions they personally think might lead to improvement. For example, it's likely the educators in this room feel different levels of responsibility for student learning, even though this is a major point of the statement. Part of the reason Sofia is sharing the system's theory of action is to surface these differences so that the participants can all begin to generate a common answer to the question that is on many of these educators' minds: *Why are we doing rounds?* Nevertheless, these moments can be difficult in the early months since all the educators bring their personal theories with them and these don't always agree with others in the room.

After a few moments of silence, Sofia changes the slide to one that shows some misconceptions about rounds (figure 1.5). "I think that's a good segue for talking about what rounds is really for and what it's not," she says. "We all remember the old learning walks or drive-bys, when the district would come once a year or so for a couple of hours and then leave without really saying anything. In fact, I used to be on some of those walk-throughs and was in some of your schools doing that a couple of years ago." A few folks chuckle at the memory, and there's a buzz of side conversations for a couple of seconds.

Sofia continues, "Rounds are not meant to be an evaluation, and we're not here to check up on the school. We're not here to see what page of the pacing guide the teachers are on. The most important thing is that the purpose is the learning of the people in this room. Hopefully, we can also give some useful feedback to the school."

Although the detailed scene described so far demonstrates several ways in which instructional rounds differs from the learning walks that Lakeside previously used, nothing makes that clearer than when Sofia says, "The most important thing is . . . the learning of the people in this room." In other words, Sofia is more interested in what this group of people learns today than she is in telling Jefferson High what it should or should not be doing about its problem of practice. *Unfortunately, none of the people in the room have any reason to believe Sofia when she says this.* This is not because the educators view Sofia as untrustworthy. In fact, Sofia is quite well-liked and respected by all of the educators with whom I spoke. Nevertheless, they have little reason to trust the rounds process—yet—because their previous experiences with Lakeside's other school improvement processes

---

**FIGURE 1.5**

## What rounds is *not*

Rounds is not:

- "Walkthroughs" or "drive-bys"
  - Rounds is descriptive, analytic, inferential

- A teacher evaluation tool
  - No assessment of individual teachers
  - Separate the person from the practice; focus on the practice

- An implementation check
  - Rounds focuses on patterns of practice, not compliance with directives

- Training for supervision
  - Rounds focuses on collective learning, rather than individual supervisory practice

- A program or a project
  - Rounds is a practice, designed to support an existing improvement strategy at the school or system level

---

*Lakeside Public Schools' explanation for "what rounds is not."*

Source: The explanation was adapted from materials developed at the Instructional Rounds Institute at the Harvard Graduate School of Education.

weren't often about the learning of adults. Some of the people in the room are still expecting that there will be an evaluation of the school (or its teachers) at the end of today, but Sofia is going to ask them to do something quite different.

Sofia continues, "I want to push us because we're getting a little bit behind, and we still need to look at the school profile and problem of practice. Can you all take out the problem of practice from your folders?" She clicks the PowerPoint to the next slide, which reads: "Problem of practice. What questions do you have about the problem of practice and our focus of observation today?"

For the first time today, Karen raises her hand. She's responsible for all of the high schools in Lakeside and attends most of the network rounds visits that I've attended so far this fall.

"I'm interested in this idea in here where you've said, 'With our growing population of English language learners, it is becoming more and more difficult to move beyond comprehension and into inference, analysis, and synthesis.' Just wondering what your percentages of English language learners are this year and what the ELA [English language arts] results looked like for that group last year."

James refers the group to the Jefferson School profile, where last year's tenth-grade test results in ELA, math, and science are disaggregated along a number of dimensions (table 1.1 shows the data for ELA).

"I think we're up to about twelve percent this year," he says, "and only about four percent of those students tested as proficient in ELA last year. You'll also see that we had a big drop in the number of proficient students from 2009 to 2010. I think that was the most frustrating part for our English teachers because they worked really hard last year, and we got them some professional development they wanted and some more resources. But we had some staff turnover at the ninth and tenth grades last year, and I think that might have hurt us."

Mike, a science teacher from the visiting Emerson School raises his hand.

"Go ahead, Mike," says Sofia.

"Have your different departments tried really focusing on the vocabulary they need? I mean really focusing on academic language and vocabulary. I think that's the biggest obstacle for most of these kids."

Tricia, an English teacher at Jefferson, jumps in. "You mean like word walls? Yeah, we've been doing that, but lots of them are so low-level, particularly the level two ELLs [English language learners], but I'm not sure what they're doing in the level one classes. Most of those kids don't really read or write any English at all when they first come in."

Sofia wants to get the participants into classrooms in the next ten minutes, and she chimes in now. "Are there other questions about the problem of practice?"

## TABLE 1.1

### STUDENT PERFORMANCE DATA, JEFFERSON SCHOOL, GRADE 10, ENGLISH LANGUAGE ARTS

| Performance level | 2007 | 2008 | 2009 | 2010 |
|---|---|---|---|---|
| Advanced | 0 | 0 | 2 | 1 |
| Proficient | 18 | 28 | 42 | 21 |
| Needs improvement | 50 | 54 | 39 | 63 |
| Failing | 32 | 17 | 17 | 15 |

Dave asks, "So, you want us to observe what kind of scaffolding teachers are using, right? I just want to make sure that I'm focusing on what will be helpful to the school."

Tricia responds, "I mean, looking at the scaffolding will be helpful. But also, what are teachers asking kids to do, and what kind of supports is the teacher providing? Like graphic organizers or manipulatives or whatever."

"Like models or something hands-on?" Dave asks.

"Well," Tricia says, "you probably won't see models in the English classes, but the teacher might have a map or a picture or something that could serve the same purpose."

"Got it," he says. "That's helpful."

"Wait, but what if the teacher isn't using any of those?" asks another Emerson teacher. "I thought we weren't checking on whether they were using something specific."

"Just write what you think the task is then," James says.

"Am I allowed to talk to the kids?" asks Tricia.

Although time is running short this morning, Sofia lets this conversation run for a few more minutes. The host school has provided a problem of practice that is supposed to focus the group's work today; the clarification of that problem is important so that everyone understands the nature of the host school's problem. In fact, this process of asking questions usually ends up clarifying the problem for the host as much as it clarifies it for the visitors.

Sofia jumps back in. "We're going to talk about some of the classroom observation norms," she says. "And I think the next part will be helpful for explaining what Tricia and Dave are talking about. Can I go on to the next slide?"

"Yeah, sorry, just go on," says Tricia.

"No, I'm glad you asked. That's really what this next part is about."

## A Typical Plan for Classroom Observations

In Lakeside, classroom observations consist of four 20-minute observations, always in teams of four or five. The host schools vary how they schedule groups for observations: some schools prefer that no two groups see the same classroom, while others purposely schedule groups so that the groups do see some of the same classrooms. Table 1.2 is the schedule for this particular day, a typical design that I encountered.

| TABLE 1.2 | | |
| --- | --- | --- |
| **CLASSROOM OBSERVATION SCHEDULE** | | |
| Team 1 | Team 2 | Team 3 |
| 8:25–8:45 Mr. Bass, Rm 202 | Ms. Renault, Rm 211 | Ms. Bryant, Rm 215 |
| 8:50–9:10 Ms. Fink, Rm 210 | Mr. Jones, Rm 204 | Ms. Renault, Rm 211 |
| 9:15–9:35 Ms. Progo, Rm 108 | Ms. Alicea, Rm 102 | Ms. Ortiz, Rm 101 |
| 9:45–10:05 Ms. Ortiz, Rm 101 | Mr. Sinclair, Rm 118 | Ms. Progo, Rm 108 |

*A typical classroom observation schedule for rounds in Lakeside Public Schools. Note that some teachers were observed by more than one observation group on this day.*

Before the participants leave with their observation groups, Sofia gives the educators one more slide with the directions for what they should do when they enter classrooms today (figure 1.6).

She explains, "Before we get into our observation groups, I want to go over some things for observing in classrooms. First, let's practice describing what we see using these image cards."

Sofia gives one card to each person in the room and asks the person not to show it to anyone else. The cards have pictures of animals, people, or scenes full of colorful objects. She asks the participants to find a partner and describe the card

| FIGURE 1.6 |
| --- |
| **Reminders for classroom observations** |
| **Observation norms:** Fine to ask students questions when it seems appropriate. Refrain from talking to each other in classrooms. <br><br> **Reminders:** Describe what you see. What is the task? What are students saying and doing? What are teachers saying and doing? Be specific. Pay attention to the instructional core (teacher, student, content) and the evidence related to the problem of practice. |

*Lakeside Public Schools' rounds network offered these guidelines before rounds to remind educators how to observe in the classroom.*

to that person for a couple of minutes. Then, the participant shows the card to the partner person, discuss the image together for a minute, and then switch turns. The purpose of this exercise is for one person to practice describing something to someone who can't see what is being described. This skill becomes important later, when these educators share their observation data with one another and try to make sense of the data as a group.

"It's almost time for us to get into classrooms," Sofia says, "so let's go over some final details. If you're not sure what to write down when you're in the classroom, just keep in mind those two focus questions in the problem of practice that the school gave us: 'How are teachers scaffolding instruction to prepare *all* students for higher-level critical thinking skills required for Honors, AP, and the SAT? How are *all* students responding to the content and current task?'"

Sofia continues, "I know sometimes when I'm observing and there's a lot going on in the classroom and I kind of get lost for a minute, I just try to remember, 'What is the task? What are students saying and doing? What are teachers saying and doing?' Be specific, and try to pay attention to the instructional core, not what you see on the walls or something like that. After the first observation, we're going to do one hallway calibration. Dave, can you lead that in your group?"

"Sure," Dave says. "Do you mean like talking about what we saw after the first classroom observation?"

"Yeah, so that you can check each other for judgmental language. If you hear something that sounds like it's judgmental, you should ask each other, 'What is the evidence that makes you say that?' You shouldn't discuss the data more than a couple of minutes. Just describe what you saw, and you shouldn't debrief in the hallway after any of the other observations. Does everyone have a copy of the observation schedule?"

"Let's get into observation groups then," Sofia continues. "I'll take team one, and whatever four people want to come. Dave, why don't you take team two and three other people. James, you'll lead group three.

"Actually," James says, "I need someone else to lead the group because I'll need to step out for a meeting for ten minutes during second period."

"Oh, OK," Sofia says. "No problem. Tricia, can you take that group?"

"Yeah, I think I can handle it."

"Great," Sofia says. "Thanks."

Sofia, Karen, two teachers, and an observer (me) constitute group 1. After a quick check that everyone has paper to write on, the group heads down the hallway to Mr. Bass's ninth-grade English class.

## CHAPTER 2

# What Did We See?

## Managing the Debrief

The obscure we see eventually.
The completely obvious, it seems, takes longer.

—*Edward R. Murrow*

After the last classroom observation of the morning, the three teams regroup back in the conference room. Although Sofia will give them all the same general instructions, each team will process its classroom observation data in very different ways. In this chapter, we'll focus on how two of the groups process their data and how Sofia manages them. As we'll see, the groups each come to similar conclusions at the end of the day, but take very different routes for getting there.

Sofia has projected a slide on a wall at one end of the room (figure 2.1). The slide gives instructions for the descriptive part of the debrief; in addition to *description*, a debrief includes a series of other steps: *analysis, prediction,* and *the next level of work*. Figure 2.1 asks each individual to spend some time on his or her own looking back over notes and working silently. Part of Sofia's purpose for asking the participants to write their data on sticky notes is to give each person time to think about which observations seem most closely related to the problem of practice or are critical to the discussion. Another reason is that these notes can later be organized in a variety of ways that allow each observation group to tell a story about what they saw today. We'll look in on two of those groups now as they work through the protocols.

---

**FIGURE 2.1**

## The Descriptive Process

**Descriptive debrief**

*On your own:*

- Read through your notes.
- Star data that seems relevant to the problem of practice and/or data that seems important.
- Select 10–15 pieces of data and write each one an individual sticky note.
- Place sticky notes on chart paper.

*With your group:*

- Help each other stay in the descriptive (not evaluative) voice. "What did you see/hear that makes you think that?"
- Everyone speak once before anyone speaks twice.
- Remember that this work is "messy."

---

*Lakeside Public Schools' instructions for the descriptive stage of instructional rounds.*


## OBSERVATION GROUP 1

This small group of four includes Dave, James, and one teacher each from the Jefferson and Emerson High Schools. Dave has some experience with instructional rounds, and Sofia has asked him to be a facilitator in the group if she's busy supporting other groups in the room. The last line of the slide—"Remember that this work is 'messy'"—is validated somewhat as the three observation teams begin to organize and finish their lunch. Most of the people in Dave's group are reading through their observation notes now, and Dave is starting to transfer some of his observations to yellow sticky notes.

A few minutes after 11 a.m., Sofia gives the room a time-check. "You should be finishing up your sticky notes and starting to put them up on the chart paper," she says. "You'll want to save enough time so that everyone can read their sticky notes for your group." Dave gets up and places six sticky notes on the chart paper, rearranges the order, and then steps back to look at what he's done. There isn't a right way of doing this, but he's the first to put anything up on paper. After he sits down, he looks around at everyone else still writing. He reaches for a pad of sticky notes and starts to write again.

By 11:10, everyone in Dave's group is standing around a piece of chart paper that is stuck on the wall and full of yellow sticky notes. One of these sticky notes says:

---

**Class #1**

The teacher asked a student to repeat the directions for the class. When the student didn't know all of the directions, she asked a second student to help him. The second student said: "I have a question about what metaphors and simile mean. Can we talk about that first?"

---

Each of the members of Dave's group reads his or her sticky notes aloud, one by one. When Dave reads the sticky note about similes and metaphors, one of the teachers says, "I heard that, too. I had an observation about the similes and metaphors as well." She points to the chart paper, where the following sticky note is posted:

---

**Class #1**

The teacher explained metaphors and similes to a group of students near the front. She said, "Similes use 'like' or 'as' to make a comparison. Metaphors make a comparison but they don't use 'like' or 'as.'"

---

For the next ten minutes, the participants in this group finish reading their sticky notes aloud. Occasionally, Dave or another teacher will ask a point of clarification, but mostly, people just listen in this group. The observations are descriptive, but often describe what seems like the same event from different perspectives, like a movie shot from different camera angles.

When Sofia puts her hand up to quiet the room a few minutes later, there's a new slide projected on the wall. The participants all turn from the chart paper to look at the next set of instructions (figure 2.2).

In each small group, there's at least one person who has been through this process before. At the moment, Dave is suggesting to his group that they classify the sticky notes into three broad categories: students, teachers, and content. James says, "I don't think that really goes in 'students.' It's kind of both 'students' and 'content.' There's a lot of the stickies that don't really fit into one category."

"It's just a way to look for patterns," says Dave. "We can change it if we don't like it."

"Yeah, but I'd rather not have to start over," says the Emerson teacher. "Can we add a few more categories for some of these? Maybe one that's about different kinds of instruction?"

"Do you mean like direct instruction versus student-centered?" James asks.

"Well, that, plus maybe differentiated instruction. I know their problem of practice said something about differentiated instruction."

---

**FIGURE 2.2**

## The analysis

### Analysis

Analyze the descriptive evidence in your small group, group sticky notes, and label groupings.

- A sticky note can stand alone. A sticky note can be duplicated.
- What patterns do you see?
- What groupings help you make sense of what you see?

### Reflection

- What difference does sticking to evidence make in your conversations?
- What is challenging for you?

*Lakeside Public Schools' instructions to educators for the analysis stage of instructional rounds.*

"That's true," says Dave. "But it also wants us to look at higher-order thinking. I wonder if there is a way to include that information on the chart."

"That's a good idea," James says. "Let me see what you guys think about this. I'm imagining a grid."

For the next few minutes, the group discusses the names of the categories it will use for the grid and places the sticky notes into those categories. After about fifteen minutes, the notes have been sorted onto a grid on the chart paper (figure 2.3).

On the left side of the chart paper are two categories: "lower-order thinking" and "higher-order thinking." Along the top are the words "task," "students," and "teachers." The majority of the sticky notes fall into the lower portion of the grid, which corresponds to what this group calls "lower-order thinking skills."

## OBSERVATION GROUP 2

Across the room, Tricia's group is also trying to organize its data into categories, but is having trouble categorizing their observations. The group members agree that there should be a category called "task," but aren't sure where to place some of the other data they have. For example, several members of the group have recorded snippets of conversation between a teacher and students, and they aren't sure whether these should have their own category or be folded into some other category. In the end, they decide to leave some of their work uncategorized and focus on two categories: task and dialogue. They seem glad to have something down on paper, but are also unsatisfied with the chart (figure 2.4). One of the teachers remarks, "I'm not sure we did this right."

Sofia now joins this group. The same teacher again says, "I'm not sure we did this right."

Sofia doesn't think there's a right way of doing this, except to stay focused on the evidence that they have before them. She's going to push this teacher (and her group) to focus on what they *did* see, rather than what they might have *expected* to see. This is a difficult habit for all educators to break, but one that's important for generating an accurate account of what's actually happening across classrooms.

Sofia says, "There's no right way to organize the data. I'm curious about this sticky note right here under 'extra thoughts' that says, 'there weren't any objectives.'"

The same teacher responds, "I didn't see any objectives on the board, and three of the kids didn't have anything on their desk."

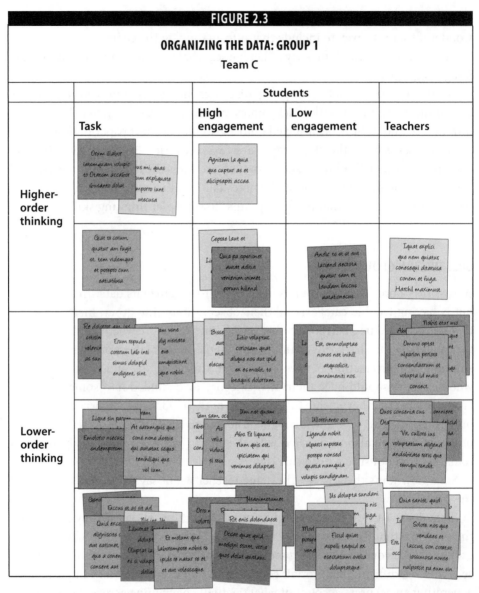

**FIGURE 2.3**

**ORGANIZING THE DATA: GROUP 1**

Team C

|  | | Students | | |
|---|---|---|---|---|
| | **Task** | **High engagement** | **Low engagement** | **Teachers** |
| **Higher-order thinking** | | | | |
| **Lower-order thinking** | | | | |

*Each rounds group organizes its sticky notes on chart paper during the analysis stage of instructional rounds. Group members are free to develop categories and groupings in any way they wish. Above, this observation team has created a display with the categories "Lower-order thinking" and "Higher-order thinking" along the left side and the headings "Task," "Students," and "Teachers" along the top. Note that the large majority of the sticky notes appear in the lower half of the chart, representing what this group calls lower-order thinking.*

## FIGURE 2.4

### ORGANIZING THE DATA: GROUP 2
#### Team A

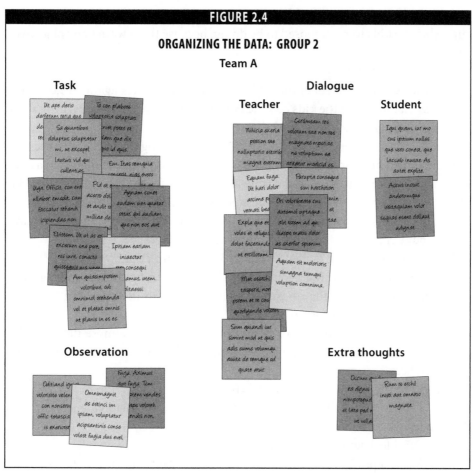

Each rounds group organizes its sticky notes on chart paper during the analysis stage of instructional rounds. Participants are free to develop categories and groupings in any way they wish. This observation team has created a display with the categories "Task," "Dialogue," "Observation," and "Extra Thoughts." One important difference between this display and group 1's display is that this team has not articulated a relationship between thinking skills and the sticky notes and is still thinking about a category they call "Extra Thoughts."

"OK, so that sticky note says what you didn't see. Can you say what you saw instead?"

"What do you mean?"

"Was there anything you noticed about what some of the kids had on their desks?" Sofia asks.

"I think some of them had a copy of the book they were reading. But I wasn't sure what the kids were supposed to be doing, because there wasn't any objective," she says again.

"Right. But, what did you see the kids doing?"

The teacher's face is reddening a bit now, and Sofia starts again, "I noticed in that class that fifteen of the kids had the book on their desk and were writing about similes and metaphors on the worksheet."

"Yeah, I saw that, too," says the teacher. "The boys along that side wall were talking about the homework for another class, and I think only one of them had a book out. The teacher spent most of the time at one of the front tables of students. She was trying to explain the difference between metaphors and similes."

The other teacher in the group has been actively biting her lip, and she now says, "Right, but I'm not sure those kids understood the difference."

Sofia asks, "What's the evidence that makes you think that?"

"Well, she said something about using 'like' or 'as' in figurative language, and one of the kids thought that meant that similes have to use the word 'like' and metaphors have to use the word 'as.'"

"Great. Can you use that information now to give a little more detail to that category you're calling 'other thoughts'? It seems like there's some important evidence in there."

"Yeah, but the sticky note I wrote is wrong, right?"

"You can always take it down or change it if you have other evidence you want to include."

"Oh. OK. I feel better. This is stressful."

There's also a process of editing and revision here, akin to editing the film from several different cameras into one story. Each observer has his or her own reel of film—a particular mental model of what was recorded—and so the team has to negotiate with one another what parts of the story get to stay and what will end up on the cutting room floor. Some data turn out to be less important than others for telling that story. And, there's a sense of initial dissatisfaction with the quality and amount of the data—most of the observers in this group say they would probably observe differently the next time, in light of their experience with the debrief so far.

## MAKING PREDICTIONS

After each group completes this stage of organizing the data into categories or patterns, Sofia projects another slide on the wall (figure 2.5). At 12:00, Sofia asks the

FIGURE 2.5

## Making predictions about student learning

**Predictions**

Predict what students are learning.

- If you were a student at this school and you did everything you were expected to do, what would you know and be able to do?

*Lakeside Public Schools' instructions to educators for the predictive stage of instructional rounds.*

groups to make predictions about what students are learning on this particular day. The slide she has projected on the wall asks the question "If you were a student in this school and you did everything you were asked to do, what would you know and be able to do?"

This stage of the process seems to activate more questions in the group than either the description or the analysis. For example, one educator asks, "Do you mean we should predict in each class what kids are learning, or across classrooms?" Another educator asks, "Should we have a particular kid in mind? I think it depends on what kid you are in different classrooms." To both questions, Sofia explains that the small group should decide whether it wants to make predictions classroom by classroom or in a more general way. The principal of the host school says that he would prefer that the group members "try to make predictions across classrooms, rather than going classroom by classroom." This seems to satisfy most folks in the room, although some would have preferred to make more specific classroom predictions about what the kids were learning. How the group makes predictions is less important than making sure everyone understands what's happening here. On one hand, going classroom by classroom tends to allow the groups to make numerous predictions about what they think kids are learning. On the other hand, making a couple of broader predictions based on the patterns of instruction across several classrooms probably gives the school more leverage for affecting classroom instruction across the school and tends to feel less like an evaluation of individual teachers. Of course, neither approach is really an evaluation of instruction; rather, each is a hypothesis based on numerous individual points of data.

Over the next fifteen minutes, there is much less writing on chart paper and much more conversation in the room. Each small group is supposed to prepare to share their analysis and predictions with the whole group. Sofia is going to record these predictions onto a document she intends to leave with the host school. Most of the small groups don't write anything the first ten or twelve minutes, and then they record their predictions in a flurry of activity in the last few minutes before time is up. This stage of the process seems quite difficult for people to complete the first time, and most resist writing anything down until they are almost out of time. One teacher explains this feeling: "It just seems premature to make any predictions after one day of observations. But, I guess we need to start somewhere."

What a regular practitioner of rounds knows—and what this particular teacher doesn't—is that this is why it's important to think of rounds as a process, rather than an event. It probably *is* premature to make a prediction about student learning in this school, if rounds is conducted only once this year. But if the process occurred repeatedly and was based on the regular observation of classroom data, the participants would probably grow more fluent and comfortable with their predictions over time. Of course, this is Sofia's point, but it's hard to understand that until one has experienced it.

## THE NEXT LEVEL OF WORK

At 12:30, Sofia projects the last set of instructions for the day (figure 2.6). The last stage of instructional rounds asks the small groups to offer suggestions of improvement to the host school. If the prediction stage feels premature to some people, the next level of work is incredibly difficult because it asks people to put themselves in

---

**FIGURE 2.6**

### Making suggestions for the next level of work

**Next level of work**
- Focused feedback: state 3–4 actions—who, what, by when
- Questions are OK, but not to the exclusion of actions
- 3–4 patterns in analysis and prediction that relate to the problem of practice

*At the end of a school visit, the network members who have observed this day will make recommendations to the host school about what they might do next. Sometimes, the network members will also think about what else they need to learn or do as a group, before the next school visit.*

the place of the host school: What should the school do next? Who should do it? When should the educators do it? The three observation groups push hard for the next twenty minutes and record a number of suggestions and recommendations. For example, group 2 suggests that the host school and its teachers should "provide more opportunities for students to demonstrate higher-order thinking skills, that is, evaluating and creating." Group 3 suggests that "teachers should release responsibility to allow students to demonstrate more higher-level thinking skills."

While these statements on their face seem straightforward, it isn't at all clear exactly *how* the school should do what the groups are recommending. In other words, educators at Jefferson High School have already told the rounds network that they are interested in higher-order thinking skills. Presumably, they would be working on these skills if they knew how to do it. So, the host school may not be surprised to hear these comments—in fact, it probably confirms the problem for the school's educators, which may be helpful. But this is where Sofia's point about the learning of the group comes into play. She's more interested in having the group begin to understand and articulate, using common language, the challenges of asking teachers to ask kids to do tasks that require higher-order thinking. At this point in the process, this is more important than giving the host school some premature solutions to a problem it just started working on. At the same time, the process can feel initially unsatisfying to the host school because it really does want answers to this problem. Sofia's dilemma—and responsibility—is to figure out how long to hold people in this ambiguous, uncomfortable space while they generate common language and capacity to solve specific instructional problems related to rigor across many schools at the same time.

## WRAPPING UP AS A WHOLE GROUP

At about 1:00, Sofia brings the three small groups together for the last part of the day's process. Each group presents some of the patterns, predictions, and suggestions, while Sofia types the information into a large grid projected on the screen to capture the information in a concise form for the host principal (table 2.1). On this particular day, the groups ask clarifying questions of one another while they present, but there aren't any strong disagreements in the room during this wrap-up. For example, group 1 begins by saying, "Most of the students were engaged in remembering, understanding, and applying," which corresponds to the lower three levels of Bloom's Taxonomy of Educational Objectives. This group also

| TABLE 2.1 | | |
|---|---|---|

**CAPTURING THE DATA AND PATTERNS**
Rounds team feedback

| Evidence → pattern | Predictions<br><br>*If you were a student at this school and you did everything you were expected to do, what would you know and be able to do?* | Next level of work |
|---|---|---|
| *Group 1*<br>• Mostly engaged in remembering, understanding, and applying<br>• Lots of teacher-to-student and student-to-student collaboration using inquiry and asking why<br>• Evidence of scaffolding in all classes<br>• Technology was integrated into all of the classes, mostly re-representation of information | *Group 1*<br>• Student will be able to use technology to prepare for future learning<br>• All students will be prepared to take risks to learn new and different concepts<br>• Read and comprehend text within a specific context<br>• Students will work collaboratively together | *Group 1*<br>• Deepen the use of technology to support higher-level thinking skills<br>• Ensure that scaffolding does lead to higher-order thinking skills<br>• Ensure more student-centered work |
| *Group 2*<br>• Most tasks involve remembering, understanding, and applying<br>• A few tasks involve evaluating and creating<br>• We saw evidence of teachers using technology as a tool to support instruction | *Group 2*<br>• Students can develop an outline that will enable them to create a five-paragraph essay with a thesis statement, supporting evidence, and a conclusion<br>• Students can compile evidence to support an argument or a viewpoint | *Group 2*<br>• Teachers need to provide more opportunities for students to demonstrate higher-order thinking skills, i.e., evaluating and creating<br>• Teachers need to do whole-class "check-ins" that involve/engage all students |
| *Group 3*<br>• Scaffolding is widespread and geared mostly toward lower-order thinking skills—some evidence of scaffolding for higher-order thinking<br>• Students are asked to read, annotate, find/highlight, and in some cases interpret evidence<br>• All students were engaged, some passively, some actively | *Group 3*<br>• Students can, with scaffolding, annotate a text—some show evidence of doing so independently<br>• Students can follow an outline and identify related evidence when given the associated framework<br>• Students can use a teacher-generated formula or outline to write an essay/research paper | *Group 3*<br>• Teachers need to release responsibility to allow students to demonstrate more higher-level thinking skills<br>• Consider how to push all students to higher levels of thinking despite high variability in current student ability/engagement<br>• Consider systemic/schoolwide strategies for differentiated learning opportunities for students |

*Lakeside Public Schools always leaves a summary of the evidence, patterns, predictions, and recommendations for the next level of work for the host school.*

predicts that students would be able to "read and comprehend texts within a specific context." Group 2 has similar patterns in its data. Its presentation begins with "most tasks involved remembering, understanding, and applying." This group also predicts that students would be able to "develop an outline" for a five-paragraph essay. Each group has a number of other patterns and predictions, but all three groups identify a pattern of students using "lower-order thinking skills" across the classrooms they observed. This observation stands, despite each group's observing in different classrooms and deciding to organize the data in very different ways.

At the close of the day, Sofia also asks that the principal of the host school be in touch with her within two weeks about how the school intends to follow up on the data. She gives the host principal several copies of a document that provides several options for the host school to build on the observation data and recommendations that it has received today (figure 2.7). For example, Jefferson's principal might continue the rounds process with just the educators in his school and build on their experience today. Or, he might use the recommendations for the next level of work to design a specific professional development session around the patterns collected during today's classroom observations.

## MANAGING THE DEBRIEF: SOME LESSONS

One might at first be disappointed to learn that the rounds network didn't solve Jefferson's problems today. It appears that the visitors have left the host school with a great deal of information, and as many questions as answers. However, it was never Sofia's intent for the network to solve these problems today; rather, her main goal for the group was that they would learn something from one another. One might also at first be disappointed that neither Sofia nor Karen provided a summation or judgment of the school at the end of the session. As an illustration of this point, one educator pulled me aside at the end of this day of rounds to ask, "So, what did you really think of the school? I know we're not supposed to judge, but what did you really think?" Of course, this was also not Sofia or Karen's intent, but the educator's comment reflects a strong culture of schools that often prefers rank or position over process. This is not easily unlearned in one day. More generally, the participants in this session learned that educators can develop some common understanding about what they are seeing across classrooms in a school or system, but that this takes many hours of in-depth discussion and analysis of the data with a skilled facilitator who understands how to get educators to describe what they saw using specific, nonjudgmental language.

---

### FIGURE 2.7

## What happens after a school visit?

**Four instructional rounds follow-up options**

1. Do rounds at your school to gauge student learning and growth

2. Describe follow-up for "Next Level of Work": PD [professional development], Common Planning Time, research, timelines, outcomes, expectations, assessment

3. Develop a plan with another school to cross-pollinate your next level of work through either of the following:
   • Select a school that has a similar POP [problem of practice] focus question and collaborate
   • Offer support to a school that has a POP focus question in which you have demonstrated strength

4. School-based option

| Problem of practice: | | | | |
|---|---|---|---|---|
| Select option: | | | | |
| Action step(s) | Team or person responsible | Timeline | Resources needed | Evidence of implementation and next action steps |
| | | | | |
| | | | | |

*One of the ongoing questions about instructional rounds in Lakeside Public Schools and in many other school systems is what the host school and network are supposed to do after it is over. Lakeside gives the host schools four follow-up options.*

These educators also learned something about Jefferson (and each other) while working with one another. In particular, they learned that there is a common instructional pattern across Jefferson's classrooms, even though the groups took very different routes to arrive at that conclusion. At the same time, many of the participants were not necessarily satisfied with the patterns and recommendations they generated. And they all left the room mentally fatigued. In short, convincing the group that this process might be worth doing on a regular basis is no easy task.

This detailed example of the instructional rounds process illustrates various immediate reasons why the process is initially difficult and maybe even unpleasant for some educators. The reasons include previously poor experiences with learning walks and other classroom observation programs; a lack of common language or understanding of instructional problems; and especially an infrequent emphasis on the learning of adults in the system and on processes like rounds, where that learning is supposed to happen.

These are the immediate reasons why educators might not initially find instructional rounds to be a pleasant experience. But we are still left with Sofia's more fundamental questions: how will the system encourage educators to adopt this learning process on a *regular* basis? And what kind of bigger problems will the system encounter along the way while making that shift from triage to learning? These more fundamental questions about Lakeside and rounds will dominate the rest of this book.

## CHAPTER 3

# Why Rounds?

## Developing a Theory of Action

In theory, there is no difference between theory and practice.
But, in practice, there is.

—*Often attributed to Yogi Berra*

Sofia has a theory. It's an untested, preliminary one at this point; nevertheless, it's a theory about why she's leading instructional rounds. She wants the network to focus on its own learning, rather than try to fix a school or its students, and she wants the learning to contribute to a common understanding of the instructional problems faced across the system. She has an initial theory that instructional rounds can help the schools, and it goes something like this: "If we practice instructional rounds in every high school, then over time we'll be able to focus more on the learning of everyone, rather than just the deficits of students."

The role of theories of action in school improvement varies greatly, but has steadily grown in importance and visibility, at least if one considers the more frequent appearance of these theories in American school systems. In their work on the learning of organizations, Chris Argyris and Donald Schön showed how theories of action could be useful tools for examining the gap between the stated and the actual ways that organizations (or individuals) act on their ideas.[1] Theories of action also play a major role in how Elizabeth City and colleagues describe the instructional rounds process. In their book, they encourage facilitators of instructional rounds to develop theories of action and test those theories against their colleagues' ideas about how rounds might lead to improvement. It's not surprising, then, that Sofia and the rest of Lakeside Public Schools have also begun to develop theories of action, and this provides us with a case for understanding *why* educators think it's important to practice rounds. As we'll see, educators in Lakeside don't necessarily agree on a purpose for rounds until after they have been practicing it for some time. Even then, it turns out that continuing to get feedback on and revise a theory of action is a major part of the practice of improvement and the way that Lakeside responds to the question "Why are we doing rounds?" In this chapter, we'll look at two different ways to distribute, get feedback on, and revise a theory of action as part of the practice of instructional rounds.

Importantly, not all school systems have a theory of action. Some school systems that practice instructional rounds don't have a theory of action. And many school systems that have a theory of action do not practice instructional rounds. More generally, how other school systems develop and share their theories of action varies greatly, regardless of whether they are currently using instructional rounds. However, Lakeside's theory of action, and Sofia's protocol for sharing it, gives us an opportunity to examine how the educators in the system understand the superintendent's vision and the steps that lead to that vision. Lakeside has provided us with a hypothesis about how it intends to improve, and we can listen to educators respond to that statement.

The superintendent's theory of action is also not necessarily the same one that other educators will understand or put into practice. For example, each educator who is asked or required to participate in the network brings a great deal of experience with previous improvement programs that influence how they view instructional rounds. Each educator who participates has his or her own personal theories about what kind of action might lead to improvement. These individual theories often differ from those of the superintendent's office. In this sense, the Lakeside school system is not unusual. Sofia and her colleagues haven't miscommunicated the system's theory of action; rather, these differences are a natural result of distributing information to numerous busy professionals who have to pay attention to several (sometimes competing) messages from both within and outside the system about what they should be doing.

Also recall that Sofia's more fundamental dilemma is how to manage the transition to the adult learning process that is rounds, across the Lakeside school district. Sofia wonders how the system will encourage educators to adopt this learning stance on a more regular basis. We need to keep this question in mind as we listen to educators talk about the system's theory of action, because it will inform the options the Lakeside leadership has for promoting and supporting the kind of learning that Sofia and her colleagues intend.

## SHARING AND REVISING A THEORY OF ACTION: A PROTOCOL

As we saw in chapter 1, Lakeside has a theory of action, which Sofia shares at the beginning of each network visit. It's a causal statement about some ideas Lakeside has for improvement and the impact it expects on instructional practice and student performance. Using an *if-then* construction, this statement outlines Lakeside's best ideas (at the moment) about how the system will close the gap between its current state and the superintendent's goals of "ensuring proficiency" and "closing achievement gaps." At the beginning of the day, Sofia produces a copy of the theory of action for each participant and uses a simple protocol to lead a discussion of it (see exhibit 3.1, "A Protocol for Sharing and Revising a Theory of Action").

The network members spend a few minutes reading and responding to Lakeside's theory of action, talking in pairs about what they've read, and then have a large group discussion about it. Educators can suggest revisions to the statement, while district office personnel take notes and ask questions. All of this takes place before any person steps foot in a classroom to observe on a rounds day.

Taking time to read Lakeside's theory of action elicits a variety of responses from the teachers and principals who attend a day of instructional rounds. In general, people appreciate that they are being asked for their feedback about Lakeside's theory. At the same time, there are several big, abstract ideas like "effective instruction," "personal responsibility," and "achievement gap" in the statement, and these phrases create questions when Sofia shares the theory. To be sure, things like effective instruction and achievement gaps are important concepts for the district to discuss with the educators who are charged with instruction and interacting with students and families on a daily basis. But educators have different ideas about what these phrases mean and what the implications might be for their daily work.

Lakeside's theory of action is not unusual: a quick review of other school systems show that many of these organizations have theories that are quite broad. This is an important starting point; many of these statements typically start with the abstract and become more concrete after subsequent revisions. But in talking about this theory of action, educators in Lakeside tend to focus on the more abstract ideas as they try to understand the vision. For example, in chapter 1, Dave said that he thought the word *infrastructure* could mean a number of things, like

---

**EXHIBIT 3.1**

### A Protocol for Sharing and Revising a Theory of Action

*Lakeside discusses the system's theory of action at the beginning of each day of instructional rounds. The following protocol describes how Sofia typically manages that discussion.*

1. As a group, discuss the theory and purpose of instructional rounds (ten minutes). Questions that Sofia typically provides answers for:
   - Who is here?
   - Why are we all here?
   - What's the purpose of instructional rounds?
   - What's the instructional core?
   - What are the learning objectives for the group today?

2. Next, she gives each person a written copy of the district's theory of action (three minutes). Each person should read the statement and write down questions or revisions to it, directly on the paper. Guiding questions for this stage include:
   - What questions do you have about the theory of action?
   - What words or phrases would you like to discuss further?

3. Then, she asks the group to do a turn and talk (three minutes).
   - Pairs of rounds participants discuss with a partner their questions or revisions.

4. Finally, Sofia facilitates a brief discussion while pairs share their questions, revisions, or concerns (five minutes).
   - District-level staff (or other educators who represent the authorship of the theory of action) should *not* speak during this time, except to ask clarifying questions.
   - District-level staff *could* take notes about the conversation, if all participants in the room are aware of this.

---

working science labs or professional development, and he was not sure if the rounds process was another kind of infrastructure as well. Other teachers are grateful to be included in the process of providing feedback to the district office, but are occasionally skeptical about the ability of the district to deliver on the vision contained in the theory of action. One teacher refers to this as the "gap between theory and practice" that she experiences "emotionally." She wants "a team willing to have that conversation." To be sure, everyone has a slightly different idea about what the theory of action means. In fact, Lakeside's theory of action pushes on each individual's implicit, personal theories about where the district is headed and what each person's role is in that vision. In the absence of specific, concrete language about what the system is asking them to do, educators will create their own definitions for "rigorous instruction" and "personal responsibility." This is a problem because it means there are many competing visions for improvement in Lakeside, and these will need to be discussed and reconciled so that instructional rounds can be attached to a powerful theory of improvement.

## A PRINCIPAL'S VIEW

Throughout the school year, I repeatedly asked educators about the purpose of instructional rounds. I also listened to groups of educators as they discussed Lakeside's theory of action at the beginning of each day of rounds. My reason for paying attention to both was to listen to *why* they thought Lakeside was asking them to participate. In other words, when people talk about Lakeside's theory of action, do they talk about rounds? When they talk about rounds, do they have ideas about how it helps the system improve? I interviewed one experienced principal named Emily early in the year, and she gave me an overview of several different issues when I asked her why, in her opinion, Lakeside was doing rounds:

> I think they like the idea that teachers are participating in data gathering. Actually, maybe that's not something they were thinking about [at the beginning]. But I think they like the idea that principals and other professionals are talking about instruction. Specifically talking about instruction because that will help them gain information on giving schools individual information—helping them gain information on what they're looking for when they're in classrooms in terms of looking at what instruction is or what it isn't. Actually, now that the focus has been on rigor, I think their thought process is "[Rounds] will help us determine where the people are constantly looking for rigor." I also think they kind of started it and have adjusted it as they go along and see the benefits and then say, "That's the reason, too." [laughs] Does that make sense?

There are a number of improvement ideas in Emily's explanation. At the system level, she thinks rounds might help the district office focus on rigor, but she also thinks that the district is making adjustments "as they go along," suggesting a revision and repurposing of the rounds process as it rolls out into schools. I then asked her what kinds of adjustments or changes she noticed from the district office regarding the rounds process. "Well," she said, "I think they're noticing that principals . . . people in the district are talking about instruction and getting ideas to take back to their school as well. So—I think—they didn't necessarily know that would happen when they started."

Emily sees teachers as gatherers of data and explains how educators might pick up new ideas during the rounds process and take those ideas "back to their school." On a more subtle level, she also uses language to comply with the district's emphasis on rigor. For example, she describes instructional rounds as something that helps Lakeside look for the development of rigor in schools. In this way, Emily sees rounds as something that helps the district monitor another improvement idea. Although Sofia always describes rounds as a *learning process*, educators sometimes view it as a *compliance activity* in the early months of the process. This tension between compliance and learning is a huge issue in any school improvement effort, and one common to rounds in particular. Many instructional rounds facilitators represent a central office that sometimes requires schools to comply with directives. But schools and educators can't simply comply with a learning process; they will have to adopt a learning stance over time.

## A FOCUS ON ADULTS

Some teachers I spoke with found the focus on adults and adult learning during a school visit to be refreshing, and they think the purpose of instructional rounds is to look at the relationship between what adults do and student learning. Adam has been teaching in a high school for several years and explained the relationship this way: "One reason, or one benefit, I think, is going to be that it is going to encourage people to talk about what goes on in our school with a focus on what adults are doing and the type of work that adults are giving students."

However, Adam also worries about the focus on adults. He's not convinced that all of his colleagues would agree that adults are the most important part of the equation: "Rounds sort of presumes a certain belief that may or may not exist already among the staff. And that is that teachers have the most responsibility for what kind of learning happens or doesn't happen in the classroom."

Adam has his own theory about what leads to improvement (focusing on the work adults give to kids in the classroom), but he is not sure that all of his colleagues share his theory. In fact, he wonders if Lakeside's rounds process might be undermined by the different beliefs that educators have about their role in student learning. In education research, these beliefs are probably best described by something called efficacy, which refers to an educator's belief in his or her capacity to affect student learning.[2] During rounds, educators sometimes challenge one another's sense of efficacy. Adam retold the following story explaining why those conversations are sometimes difficult: "It came up yesterday, when we had the rounds. We looked at the district's theory of action on the blue handout, and the person I shared with asked me, 'Do you think this covers everything?' I knew automatically where the conversation was going from there. So, I said, 'Yeah, I do. I think it distributes responsibility where it belongs—with district staff and building staff.' And so, he said, 'What about the students? The problem I have with this is that it doesn't account for student agency and what students need to do in order to get these results.'"

Educators sometimes disagree during rounds about whether or how their teaching affects student learning. Another way of saying this is that educators in the district have different ideas about how much control or influence they have over student learning, and this directly influences their understanding of the theory of action, the purpose of rounds, and the relationship between the two. It's likely that teachers in the district differ in their levels of personal efficacy as educators, and this sometimes comes to the surface when they talk about the district's theory of action. In the example above, the educators are speaking before a day of rounds. When the teacher asked Adam the aforementioned question about student agency, Adam had anticipated this question: "So, I just spoke from the gut and said, 'I think that we actually have a lot more influence over [students] than we realize and that a lot of the moves we make matter.' The person himself acknowledged that, 'Yeah, the district's theory covers what we have control over. So we should focus on that.' Even though you're not denying the fact that kids have agency and their choices matter, this approach—placing emphasis on what adults are doing— is more effective."

Adam likely feels higher levels of self-efficacy—his belief that his teaching influences outcomes in students—than the second teacher, and this shapes how they each understand the theory of action and the purpose for rounds. Adam has some experience managing his colleagues' beliefs about their impact on student learning, and this influences his view of the round process. But the conversation illustrates that there might not be a commonly understood purpose for rounds or belief in the theory of action at this early stage of the process, given the different beliefs educators hold about the effects of their own instruction.

## A TEACHER'S HEALTHY SKEPTICISM

In general, the more experience that people have with rounds, the more articulate and optimistic they are about the impact it might have on their teaching and student learning. Both Adam and Emily have been on rounds visits several times, are mostly optimistic about the process, and are leading groups of teachers on rounds in their respective schools. Both educators see some benefit of instructional rounds and believe that their personal theories are compatible with the process.

But other educators withhold enthusiasm for rounds and the district's theory of action for one very rational reason—they are not convinced that Lakeside will still be using the rounds process five years from now. As a result, they don't see why they should commit to rounds now. I asked Jenny, a ninth-grade teacher who has been teaching for almost ten years, about the purpose of rounds. Jenny explained: "For me personally? I don't know. This is my ninth year in [the district], and it kind of feels like, 'OK, this is what we're doing now.' And I've seen that happen, I don't know, maybe four times. And I think nine years is a really short period of time for there to be that kind of—revamping. It kind of feels like to me it's trendy."

Jenny is quite clear that she does not have a good sense of the purpose of rounds. And for her, any idea of a district theory of action has been overwhelmed by a feeling that the system's improvement ideas change too often to be useful. In fact, she calls rounds "trendy," suggesting a flavor-of-the-month approach to improvement. I asked her to try to name some of the other improvement efforts of which she has been a part. "I know one of them was Readers and Writers Workshop," she said. "And I like Readers and Writers Workshop—a lot. I think it's a great program and I learned a lot by learning it and being in the district push for it. But then I kind of see it having been let go. There are some teachers that I come into contact with now, and they don't know what it is. So, it's like I and a bunch of other people learned something, and we all got a lot of expensive training for it, and then I don't know what happened. But it went away or whatever."

As Jenny talked in more detail, she compared her experience with rounds with other instructional programs she has learned throughout the years. Readers and Writers Workshop is a specific instructional approach to teaching reading and writing. The approach takes time to learn, initially requires lots of support to be effective, and is a huge cultural shift for some teachers to implement: students work in groups organized by reading interest and level, discuss their reading in groups, confer with the teacher about their work, and edit each other's writing, as the teacher acts as facilitator of a number of activities that might be happening simultaneously in the classroom. Jenny continued: "I'll continue to participate [in rounds] with an open mind. I will not reject the information. So far I have been able to use the information for myself for some things. But when I look at it in terms of cost and what's going into it, I don't see that would change the dropout rate as drastically as something else might."

Her explanation is helpful to us in at least two ways. First, she compares rounds to an instructional program, even though Sofia has tried to make clear that rounds "isn't a program or project." It's often difficult for teachers to understand how a process (rounds) that does not provide them with immediately useful instructional strategies could be important for them or the district to learn. In particular, Jenny's theory is that it won't "change the dropout rate," which is important because this is an outcome one could measure, but that differs from both Sofia's interest in adult learning and the outcomes that are described in Lakeside's theory of action. Second, even though she has sharp criticisms for the rounds process and the district's approach to improvement, she intends to keep "an open mind" because she's been "able to use the information for myself." This is an interesting contradiction: although Jenny thinks it might be costly or wasteful for the district to engage in the rounds process widely, she thinks she is learning something useful for her classroom. In this example, we're left wondering whether she thinks her colleagues are learning something useful, and if they are, how much learning would be worth the cost of the process. Still, this educator's explanation is completely rational given her experience with change in the district. We'll need to keep Jenny's perspective in mind.

As I spent more time in the district, some educators expressed a very clear need to understand the relationship between their professional role and instructional rounds. Matt, a provider of professional development in Lakeside, described an ongoing, iterative revision of that relationship:

> I don't think that any of the [professional development facilitators] really had a very clearly articulated, firmly held theory of action. And I think that all the work together has really been, in large part, about fostering mutual understanding. You know, so it has been very helpful to hear how Sofia talks about rounds and to observe her conducting instructional rounds and for her to hear how we talk about [professional

development] and just to have conversations among the team about what this could look like. And I still don't think we have a very—a shared understanding of exactly how these two things should interface.

This educator's explanation makes a point that educators don't often express about the rounds process. By itself, rounds won't lead to improvement unless the process is tied into other existing improvement initiatives in ways that all the educators understand. Matt went on to explain what he thought it would take to make those connections more explicit: "I think at the beginning of next year we're going to be able to articulate a [new] theory of action. We'll be able to say this is exactly how we think students are going to be affected when we teach instructional rounds, when we offer professional development, and this is how we think these two things might come together. I think that's actually going to be a huge difference."

What Matt is in fact describing is a new theory of action—one that outlines the relationship between rounds and professional development sessions, rather than the more general version that currently exists. The version he imagines makes explicit how information gets shared between rounds and other professional development that is being provided across the district. He's also suggesting that his professional development team needs a theory of action—a theory subordinate to the district's, but one that will guide how the team members would do their jobs as providers of professional development.

## DEVELOPING A THEORY OF ACTION: SOME LESSONS

So what is Sofia, as a responsive rounds facilitator, to do with all of the competing visions and ideas about what Lakeside should be doing? It's clear that Lakeside's current theory of action doesn't capture everyone's interest and needs to be rewritten. In fact, the current system-level theory of action doesn't mention instructional rounds explicitly. Part of the reason for this is that only the high schools are currently practicing rounds regularly; another reason is that Sofia and Karen are still trying to figure out the purpose for rounds more generally. The subsequent versions of the theory will probably need to deal with both of these issues. One way to do that is to distribute the current version of the theory during rounds for feedback—something that Lakeside is prepared for and will continue to do. But Matt has made an interesting case and rationale for developing additional processes that describe the relationship between instructional rounds and professional development in more concrete ways.

Lakeside is beginning to articulate these relationships through visual models, rather than just written theories of action. Its view is that these models have the potential to integrate multiple programs and provide a visual representation of the relationships. This can be particularly useful in the early days of a theory of action and the rounds process, when the system doesn't necessarily know the concrete language to describe these relationships. Developing a visual representation between rounds and other things happening in the district might be a helpful intermediate stage. These models could be shared across departments and levels of the system, to more clearly answer the question "Why are we doing rounds?" For example, considering Matt's initial description above, we might imagine a preliminary model that represents an emerging relationship between the rounds process and professional development (figure 3.1).

In figure 3.1, the arrows represent theories about how information might flow in the district and could be labeled with specific terms with which educators in the system might be familiar. For example, the arrow between system-wide patterns

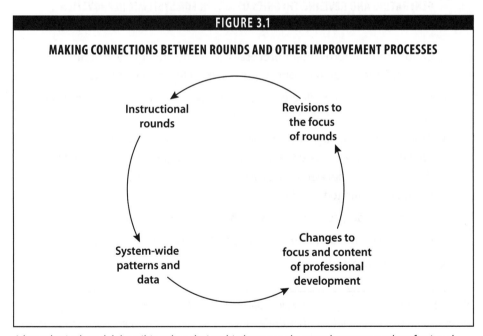

## FIGURE 3.1

### MAKING CONNECTIONS BETWEEN ROUNDS AND OTHER IMPROVEMENT PROCESSES

Instructional rounds

Revisions to the focus of rounds

System-wide patterns and data

Changes to focus and content of professional development

*A hypothetical model describing the relationship between the rounds process and professional development in a school system.*

*Source:* Adapted from materials used in Lakeside Public Schools.

and data and the changes to professional development could represent the actual instructional patterns emerging from the rounds process. Or the arrow that links changes to professional development and revisions to the focus of rounds could be labeled with the actual professional development program or focus that the system is using to increase educators' knowledge and skill. The point is that having a picture in mind can help manage expectations, particularly educators' expectations for big transitions like the learning process Sofia is managing during rounds. This model isn't a replacement for revising and sharing theories of action; rather, it could be a complement to that process—one that could be shared repeatedly across departments and levels of the system, as figure 3.2 describes.

One benefit of sharing models in this way is that it allows facilitators and leaders like Sofia to give educators a relatively concrete picture to hold on to during

---

### FIGURE 3.2

**GENERATING AND REVISING THEORIES OF ACTION FOR SYSTEMIC IMPROVEMENT: A PROTOCOL**

1. Choose three improvement processes currently under way in your system. Rounds could be one; there are likely to be many others.

2. With your colleagues, discuss why you think the processes are important and how they are related to one another.

3. Arrange these into a model of how learning happens across those processes and your system. Use arrows and/or figures to demonstrate the relationship between the processes and how information will be shared from one to the other.

4. Distribute widely to important stakeholders for feedback.

5. Use feedback to edit theories of action, strategy, and/or vision.

6. Repeat as necessary.

*It's one thing to have a theory of action. It's quite another to have educators across the system understand how instructional rounds will affect their work. This protocol can help generate those connections and create some initial understanding across the system about the role that instructional rounds might play in different departments or levels of the system.*

Source: Adapted from protocols used by the author and his colleagues at the Instructional Rounds Institute, Harvard Graduate School of Education.

the messy, early stages of rounds. As we saw in chapter 1, educators will want answers to their problems, even though that isn't the initial purpose of rounds. A process like this allows educators to understand why the system is doing what it's doing, and where the system thinks it's headed, even when there aren't very specific answers in the early stages of rounds.[3]

At the beginning of this chapter, I suggested that the answer to the question "Why rounds?" depends on whom we speak to in a school system, but that those answers would help us understand the challenges facilitators face as they manage the learning they expect to happen across a school system. One way a leader does this is by sharing and revising a system-level theory of action as part of the rounds process, as Sofia's protocol did (exhibit 3.1). But one thing we've learned along the way is that there may be other ways to make the vision for rounds more concrete for educators while a superintendent's office works on revising the theory of action. As important as it is to regularly share and revise a written theory, educators want to understand whether or how rounds will change their job. Theories of action written at the system level may be too abstract to answer those questions for each educator, but different departments and levels of the system might create models that describe these theories in more detail. Models can show specific links between rounds and other improvement processes currently happening in the system, while sharing the models regularly helps to build consensus for the broader vision. Taking the system-level theory of action and the examples of the improvement models we've just described, the idea could look something like figure 3.3.

While the system is sharing and getting feedback on the theory of action, other departments and levels of the system could be generating improvement models that describe the relationship between rounds and other processes. For example, educators who lead professional learning communities or departmental teams could build a model for how the rounds process will complement or change their work. On the other hand, curriculum coordinators and department chairs may need models that describe how they think rounds will change how educators view or understand the content that they teach. No one will know for sure if their models are robust in the early days of the rounds process, but they can serve as rationale and holding places in the short term. These models will become more accurate over time as educators provide feedback. As these models are created and shared with educators, the feedback could be used to edit the system-level theory of action. But this feedback goes both ways: as the theory is shared across the system, it should inform the models that are being created and revised in the

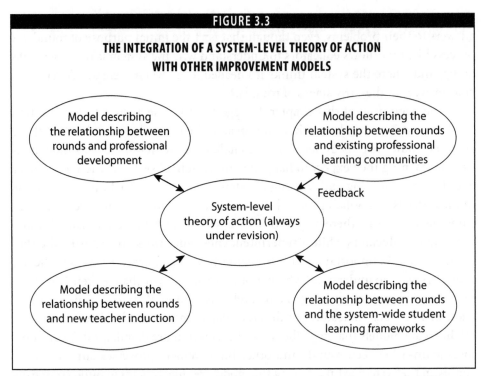

**FIGURE 3.3**

**THE INTEGRATION OF A SYSTEM-LEVEL THEORY OF ACTION WITH OTHER IMPROVEMENT MODELS**

*As educators develop models (like figure 3.2) for how instructional rounds gets integrated into the system, those models will influence—and be influenced by—the system's theory of action.*

extremities of the system. The theory guides the work, but the models that describe the rounds work make the strategies more concrete for everyone.

Regardless of how Sofia and her colleagues choose to revise their theory of action in the future, we've shown that answering the question "Why rounds?" actually helps respond to Sofia's original dilemma: how to manage a transition from triage to learning. In short, it's really about generating and revising improvement theories in ways that people can understand and act upon. A more general point emerging here is that just because educators do classroom observations together as part of the rounds process, they don't all understand or support the process in the same way. A great deal of work has to happen before and after rounds to sharpen that vision. Much of this work springs from the effort to define and refine the problem of practice, which is where we'll turn next.

## CHAPTER 4

# Whose Problem Is This, Anyway?
## Developing Problems of Practice

> Tell me to what you pay attention, and I'll tell you who you are.
>
> —*José Ortega y Gasset*

R ounds is much more than just a protocol for doing classroom observations. In fact, classroom observations are only a fraction of the work of instructional rounds. While Sofia and Karen are revising the school system's theory of action, they are also supporting each high school in the development of a problem of practice. If Lakeside Public Schools' theory of action is the *why* for rounds, then problems of practice provide the *what*—they serve as the focus of each high school's participation in the network and a statement of their struggles to educate their students. Like a theory of action, a problem of practice takes lots of time to develop outside the network visits, but are very much part of the practice of rounds. Also like a theory of action, a problem of practice requires repeated revision and retooling over time. Put another way, a large chunk of the learning that happens via instructional rounds occurs before and after a network visit, not just during classroom observations. In this chapter, we'll focus on that learning as the Lakeside high schools develop and revise their problems of practice, and we'll look at the facilitator's or another leader's role in supporting that work.

Schools and networks that practice instructional rounds use a problem of practice to focus the attention of the host school and the visiting educators as the group observes and discusses their classroom observations. Generally, the statement should focus on an instructional problem that is observable in the classroom, within the control of the educators in the school, and important to the host.[1] The statement in figure 4.1 is an example of a problem of practice from a high school in the Lakeside school system.

Each high school in the Lakeside school system developed a problem of practice in this general form: a short paragraph that provides some context, followed by one or two focus questions (figure 4.1). These statements were the basis for the classroom observations, and each was loosely tied to the system's interest in rigorous instruction. Typically, a high school developed the problem of practice with Sofia's help in the weeks leading up to the host school's rounds day. Often, members of the school's instructional leadership team would provide input during that

---

### FIGURE 4.1

## A problem of practice

Many students are able to answer simple problems, but when they are asked to answer deep or multi-step problems (such as those found in open-response exam items) they frequently shut down or give up. Many will stop reading/writing/thinking the moment they encounter a task that gives them difficulty. The support systems we create for students when they encounter rigorous work will empower them to persevere over their challenges and lead to their proficiency. These support structures will be evident in the depth of the questions both teachers and students ask, the strategies students use for answering a question they do not "understand," the methods students use to attack harder reading and writing assignments, accountable talk between students during rigorous work, and completion of longer, more difficult assignments.

**Focus questions:**

- What is the task?

- How are we encouraging students to move beyond surface-level engagement toward rigorous work with a willingness to grapple and persevere?

*A typical problem of practice for a high school in Lakeside Public Schools. These statements are used to articulate where the host school is struggling and provide a focus for classroom observations on the day the network visits the school.*

process, and many schools sought input widely from their instructional staff. But this also varied across high schools, with some principals meeting primarily just with Sofia in the week prior to the network visit. In addition, the content of the statements of the problem also varied greatly across the schools. Although most had some reference to "rigor" or "rigorous instruction," the manner in which the schools described their problems with rigor varied greatly. As a result, these problems of practice were used in different ways across the high schools in the network. The variability in problems of practice became a problem that Sofia and her colleagues had to manage throughout the year. In short, they wondered about several issues: How much should the district office be involved as a host school developed a problem of practice? How should each school's problem statement connect to the district's emphasis on rigor? And how would the system encourage the host schools to revisit and revise these statements? These questions made the work quite complicated as Sofia and her colleagues prepped thirty-eight host schools for visits; the questions had different answers on different days and in different schools. In general, Sofia thought that the district needed to provide support to high schools as they developed problems of practice, support that should diminish in quantity over time, effectively turning over the process of problems of practice development to the schools. She called this "a gradual release of responsibility" from the district to the schools. As a result, the problems described in a later section, "Early Drafts of Problems of Practice," reflect varying levels of involvement from Sofia and the district office. Sofia and her colleagues are still evaluating how to be involved in the development of problems of practice.

## THE CHALLENGES OF ARTICULATING A PROBLEM

In chapter 1 we saw that a problem of practice can activate a number of questions for both the visiting educators and the host school. In that chapter's description of rounds at a Lakeside high school, the visiting educators asked the host school for clarification about the word *scaffolding*. One educator asked, "So, you want us to observe what kind of scaffolding teachers are using, right? I just want to make sure that what I'm focusing on will be helpful to the school." These questions and conversations were common across the Lakeside district when educators discussed the problem of practice at the beginning of a day of instructional rounds. In fact, most of the host schools were still working to clarify their own language in the problem of practice up to the very minute of the classroom observations. Both the process of developing a problem of practice and the resulting product have a great deal of influence over the focus of classroom observations and the subsequent debrief of that observation data. But the act of identifying, stating, and clarifying an observable problem proves a challenge for host schools in nearly every case, and it suggests that there is something fundamentally difficult about developing a problem of practice as the basis for classroom observations.

In *Instructional Rounds*, Elizabeth City and coauthors note several typical challenges that educators face when developing a problem of practice. The authors describe situations where the host school packs too much information into the statement, essentially providing a laundry list of issues for people to observe. This makes observing carefully nearly impossible. In other examples, they describe problems of practice that serve as an audit of teachers. In that case, rounds becomes an implementation check, rather than a process of observing and learning about instruction. Other hosts might write problems of practice that provide insufficient context for outsiders to completely understand their observations.

## WHOSE PROBLEM IS THIS, ANYWAY?

All of these situations came into play at one time or another in the Lakeside school district. But the most difficult challenge among the nearly forty problems of practice in Lakeside was much more fundamental: getting educators to connect problems of student learning to the action or teaching of the adults. Most host schools were able to name a problem of student learning, but far fewer schools implicated their teaching in those student learning problems.

Lakeside is not unusual. Both at Lakeside and elsewhere, people report that identifying a problem is a huge cultural shift for the organization. In most schools, the adults are already working as hard as they can and sometimes not getting the results they want. But many educators work in a culture where admitting that one does not know what to do next is not the norm. One Lakeside teacher described this culture to me in this way: "It's hard work, and it's demoralizing if you're not having success in the classroom. So, in your frustration, you want the students to be putting more in so that you get better results. And so . . . teachers tend to . . . locate the students themselves as being the problem rather than the things [the teachers could be] doing that would improve the results."

In their early drafts many of the host schools locate the problem of practice in the students or in broader organizational or societal issues that are beyond their control. In other words, the main challenge for educators is naming a student learning problem that is under the control of the adults and might be improved if the educators learned more about their instructional practice.

This made the act of writing a problem of practice a developmental process for everyone involved in Lakeside. In the early stages of that work, the host school would typically write a draft that revealed some things it was trying to do differently and asked the observers whether they noticed the educators' new efforts in the classroom. In subsequent versions or revisions of that problem of practice, a school might cite student performance data and begin to formulate an early version of a student learning problem. With persistence and support, schools were able to name a student learning problem *and* describe teachers and administrators that were "stuck" on how to address this problem. Let's examine examples of each of these stages as they played out in Lakeside.

## EARLY DRAFTS OF PROBLEMS OF PRACTICE

In the early days of instructional rounds, most Lakeside high schools had difficulty describing a specific problem of student learning, and even more had difficulty identifying the struggles of educators who are working hard to help students improve. Instead, the host schools were likely to describe several solutions they had recently implemented, in the hopes that the rounds observers could provide feedback about whether the solution was working. Schools at this stage were likely to frame a problem of practice similar to the example below:

> [Our] students, including many of our special needs students, are out-performing their counterparts on the [state exam]. We have been able to take at-risk students with strong histories of failure to proficiency and advanced levels. We credit our teaching staff for many of these gains. Classroom observations demonstrate strong evidence of planning "high rigor" lessons. Teachers expect students to work. However, student gains are more evident in benchmark assessments and are not necessarily reflected in student grades. Attendance data and student feedback highlight a lack of active involvement and access to the curriculum by many of our students. We feel we may be working more as a filter for some to succeed rather than a pump for all to succeed.
>
> Are we reaching out to see where and when students are lost and encouraging them? Are we providing the necessary scaffolded and

targeted support for all students to experience success? Are we being flexible enough for students to experience success without coddling them?

Our efforts in attempting to answer these questions include whole school professional development regarding the relationship of high academic press with high support as a model to increase student achievement. Presently, some of our teachers are participating in a six hour mini-course geared toward addressing this issue. We hope to use this round as a means to continue the conversation.

### [Instructional Rounds] Focus Questions:
- What is the relationship between high academic press and high support in regards to student achievement?
- How does the level of the task correspond with levels of support?

The school that wrote this problem of practice is not unusual. Developmentally, this version was a typical early stage for the schools in the Lakeside district and in other places using rounds. Importantly, the problem of practice acknowledges the hard work of the educators, while suggesting (indirectly) that they have more to learn. However, this kind of framing of the problem probably makes it less likely that the observers will be able to provide large amounts of data or identify patterns of practice that will useful to the school. For example, the body of the statement contains a series of questions to which observers would only be able to answer yes or no, which may close off a range of responses that could allow for disagreement or discussion of the variation in practice. The questions "Are we reaching out . . . ? Are we being flexible . . . ?" and so on require observers to make a choice, rather than allowing them the opportunity to describe a range of practice that likely exists in the school. In addition, the statement refers to at least three issues that are not directly observable in the classroom: benchmark assessments, student grades, and attendance data. While these items may be important issues that the school is working through, they cannot be directly observed by the rounds teams in classrooms. Finally, the problem of practice suggests that professional development about the relationship between "academic press" and "support" is important to the school. However, it would probably be unclear to the visiting educators what problem of student (or adult) learning this professional development was meant to solve. Nearly all of the Lakeside high schools' early drafts of their problems of practice started in this way, because of the difficulty of developing a problem of practice.

## USING DATA: INTERMEDIATE VERSIONS OF A PROBLEM

As schools gained more experience with identifying problems and observing instruction, they were able to use data to describe problems of learning that are important to them and to describe the challenges that students face. The following problem of practice is an example of a school that has taken a step toward naming and addressing a specific problem:

> Data analysis shows that while we perform well on the [state exam], we struggle with SAT and AP scores. Through a series of focused efforts (highlighted below) we have seen our [state exam] scores steadily improve.
>
> 1. One third of students in grade 10 take both geometry and advanced algebra.
> 2. [State math exam] preparation half year or full year depending on level of need.
> 3. Cycle of Inquiry facilitated by [local non-profit] for both math and ELA teams.
> 4. Offered [state exam] boot camp in the spring of 2010.
> 5. Initiative in which all students in the warning category were given three weeks of intense math support by a knowledgeable adult (three days per week).
>
> We would like to see the same trend with both our SAT and AP scores. Presently, 9–12th grade content teams are vertically aligning curricula by backward mapping from AP courses. Teachers are beginning to understand what students need to know and be able to do by the time they are in an AP course and are adjusting accordingly. Teachers have identified the following criteria as areas of struggle for students' lack of success in AP courses: work ethic, stamina, resilience, and lack of strength in reading and writing. We have also decided to conduct a whole school implementation of three strategies (Cornell Notes, Socratic Seminar, and Costa's Levels of Questioning).
>
> [The] high school has decided to use instructional rounds as a means to delve deeper into this question. ILT [instructional leadership team] members have all received a copy of *Instructional Rounds in Education: A Network Approach to Improving Teaching and Learning* and have engaged in two rounds. The focus of rounds has been to identify what consistent strategies across grade levels and across content we do/could use to make sure students are having a rigorous experience. Through this work the ILT has developed the following definition of a culture of rigor: In a

culture of academic rigor, students create, apply, and extend knowledge that is thought provoking and personally or emotionally challenging.

**[Instructional Rounds] Focus Questions:**
- How are teachers providing consistent rigorous instruction to prepare all students for higher level critical thinking skills required for SAT and AP classes?
- What is the task?
- What are teachers doing and saying?
- What are students doing and saying?

There are some similarities between this statement and the previous example; however, at least four features distinguish this statement from the previous example and suggest that the school is in a different stage of this process. First, the school has introduced specific student data results to frame its current version of the problem statement. Second, the school has used the data to develop a preliminary statement of a student learning problem. In particular, it notes a "lack of strength in reading and writing." At the same time, the statement also locates much of the problem in the students, rather than in the organization as a whole. For example, students in this school may lack "work ethic," "stamina," and "resilience."

Third, the school has defined what it means by rigor: "In a culture of academic rigor, students create, apply, and extend knowledge that is thought provoking and personally or emotionally challenging." In addition, the focus questions at the end of the statement invite a range of responses, rather than the yes-or-no construction in the previous example. Taken as a whole, this problem of practice reflects an effort to understand a problem of student learning and puts that problem in the context of a culture of rigor that the school is working toward. Importantly, it does not describe how or why adults might have difficulty with the demands of this new instructional culture, a connection that we will explore in the next section.

## MAKING CONNECTIONS BETWEEN STUDENT AND ADULT LEARNING

Schools that regularly review the observation data from rounds visits may be able to make connections between problems of student learning and their own challenges as educators and adult learners. While examples of these kinds of problems of practice were less frequent in Lakeside, some schools had begun to make these connections. Consider this statement from a Lakeside school:

The [state exam] scores reflect that our [English language learners] are not achieving at the same level as our mainstream students. Correlation of this data with our scores shows that our ELLs are particularly not doing well in both oral and written language. This is also true for our [formerly limited English proficient] students. This is further evidenced in our analysis of both student work and grades. Observational evidence shows that these scores are a function of a lack of differentiated instruction and not enough oral language development practices.

All teachers have received ELL trainings this school year. Our focus is to have a "highly qualified" staff trained in providing the instructional strategies learned in these trainings. We believe that the strategies learned will not only serve our ELL population but all of our students, particularly in the area of academic discourse. All of our students need opportunities to participate in high-level tasks using academic language in their reading, writing, listening, and speaking.

The administrative team has engaged in two instructional rounds to investigate the role of differentiation and academic discourse in instructional practices. Evidence shows that there are varying ranges of differentiation, including an explicit focus shown through academic tasks to mostly teacher-centered classrooms with all students participating on the same tasks at the same time. In our classrooms where students are working collaboratively, there is a higher incidence of students engaging in academic discourse while in others, classroom structures emphasize the teacher asking whole class questions with some students responding. We lack a shared understanding of what higher level tasks look like in the service of having students wrestle with ideas using academic discourse. In essence, there is a lack of consistency in existing patterns of differentiation and academic discourse.

**[Instructional Rounds] Focus Questions:**
- How and at what levels are students engaging in tasks that require academic discourse?
- What is the distribution of performance on instructional tasks?

Like the previous example, this school has used specific student achievement data to describe a student learning problem, but in this case, the school implicates the organization as well as the students. In other words, the adults share the problem with the students. For example, the educators in this school "lack a shared understanding of what higher level tasks look like." While their English language learners are struggling with oral and written language, the adults are struggling with "differentiation" and "oral language practices."

It is not completely clear from the problem of practice whether the educators in the school understand the concept of differentiation in the same way, or whether they think they are using "oral language practices" in the same way. Nevertheless, the focus questions invite a variety of data from the observers, which will likely be useful to the school in making those definitions clearer. These focus questions ask *how* students are using academic discourse, and about the "distribution of performance" on tasks, allowing for description of the variation in practice that likely exists in the school.

## THREE STAGES OF PROBLEMS OF PRACTICE

Obviously, a system must attend to several issues as schools develop problems of practice across a system. There's also much for principals, teachers, and other educators in the system to learn about themselves in these examples. Despite the different ways that educators think about these problems of practice—and subsequently, the rounds process—the preceding examples allow us to trace at least three stages of development of problems of practice (exhibit 4.1).

The *initial* stage is illustrated by the idea that first drafts of problems of practice are often solutions in search of a problem. Some schools tend to present statements that aren't clear on a particular problem, but instead state a number of recent initiatives that are really solutions running unattached to a problem.

In the *emerging* stage, educators typically develop problems of practice that implicate a particular group of students. In other words, the problem is often located in students (or sometimes teachers), but the connection between the problems of student learning and those of teaching practice is relatively underdeveloped. The student learning problem is sometimes stated clearly, but without any particular ideas or statements about where adults might be struggling in their practice.

In the third, or *evolving* stage, the educators who are revising a problem of practice implicate the organization in the problem. In other words, a particular student learning problem is situated in relatively clear statements of where educators are struggling and what they may need to learn about their practice. In this way, the educators view the problem holistically and organizationally and are much less likely to locate the problem in their students. It's possible that the problem as it is currently stated is incorrect or incomplete, but educators' observations and patterns across the school will likely help inform that. Another important feature of this stage is that because it implicates the organization, it puts a healthy demand on the system (and the instructional rounds network) to provide specific support and professional development.

This three-stage process raises one other issue in the development of problems of practice: there is no such thing as the perfectly stated problem, and only the act of repeatedly observing in classrooms can help educators refine and understand

---

**EXHIBIT 4.1**

### Whose Problem Is This, Anyway?

*Recognizing the common stages of development of a problem of practice is important for both school-based leaders and system leaders. Host schools will likely need different kinds of support based on the stage of their problem of practice.*

| Stage | Characteristics | Problem located | Supports and next steps |
|-------|-----------------|-----------------|-------------------------|
| Initial | Often contains lists of recent initiatives and improvement steps already taken. | Usually not specified. Occasionally located in students. | Revise problem in light of classroom observation data. Facilitators could inquire directly about the ways in which teachers say they are struggling. |
| Emerging | Often cites student performance data but is less clear about specific teacher struggles/challenges. | Typically in students. Occasionally located in teaching practice. | Revise problem in light of most recent classroom observation data. Facilitators could ask educators to start generating theories about why the data looks like it does, and why educators might not be as effective as they would like. |
| Evolving | Describes teachers' struggles in terms of their teaching practice and connects that to specific student learning data or previous classroom observations. | In the organization. Connects teaching practice to student learning. | Facilitators could reduce their involvement. However, the school may need different professional development than other schools and targeted support based on a shifting organizational culture. |

the problem more deeply. In fact, if one were to conduct classroom observations using a stage 1 problem of practice (which many schools do), the best result is likely to be a new version of the problem of practice, rather than suggestions or actions that might lead to improvement. Another point is that the important learning in that case may not be the actual classroom visits; rather, the process of rewriting that problem of practice—in light of the observation data and patterns—would likely be far more instructive for the educators of the host school than implementing suggested changes to their practice.

This analysis leads us back to a key challenge that Sofia and other network leaders face: how to manage and support the transition from an *initial* problem of practice to an *emerging* or *evolving* problem of practice over time. Just as the rounds process uses protocols to support classroom observations, leaders could use a protocol and process for supporting what happens before and after school visits. This would allow a leader to "release responsibility" to the network participants to revise their own problems of practice, while providing them with some guidance on how to do that. So, in addition to being able to recognize and describe these stages, schools may also benefit from some ideas about what it takes to push from *initial* to *emerging*, for example.

Exhibit 4.1 shows that leaders will need to differentiate the kinds of support they provide to schools or teams that are practicing and struggling with the rounds process and the development of a problem of practice. For example, it seems clear that a school with a first draft of a problem of practice will need to rewrite that statement, but they may need support identifying data that describes student learning. Facilitators of the rounds process would also need to ask this school where they think they are "stuck." On the other hand, an *evolving* school may need specific, targeted professional development that the system hasn't typically provided in the past. This is because the school may have grown out of old professional development habits. The point here is that as the school's problem of practice changes, leaders and facilitators will need to change the manner in which they provide pressure and support to the school.

## DEVELOPING PROBLEMS OF PRACTICE: SOME LESSONS

In its most useful form, writing a problem of practice is an iterative process, particularly when the hosts are using observation data from a previous rounds visit to inform subsequent versions of the statement. As Lakeside learned over the year, individual schools need different kinds of support when developing and using a problem of practice. The school system found that it needed to differentiate the kinds of pressure and support it provided.

Like the schools at Lakeside, many other schools have difficulty identifying a problem of practice, initially locating their problems in students or in broader society. As we saw in chapter 2, educators' personal feelings of efficacy probably help explain some of the variation in how people talk about student learning and the problems they describe. All of this discussion suggests that the bulk of the learning acquired through rounds actually happens before and after the rounds visit, not just on the day of the visit itself. In other words, revising the statement in light of the most recent observation data seems to help schools move through the different developmental stages and is just as important as the actual classroom observations. "Doing rounds" might just be a fraction of the learning from which the organization would likely benefit.

If the greatest benefit from rounds derives from activities before and after rounds day, then people must participate in identifying and revising the problem of practice. In other words, the observation data (sticky notes, chart paper, recommendations) is not the professional development—instead *the discussion and revision of the problem of practice in the presence of observation data is more likely to be the work that will support improvement in the system.*

Bearing all of this in mind, let's return to Sofia's dilemma before we begin part 2 of this book: *How do we manage a transition to adult learning?* There is no doubt that managing the transition means paying attention to the processes and protocols that support learning. As we have seen, these protocols include classroom observations that are specific and nonjudgmental, at least two ways of developing and sharing theories of action so that educators begin to understand the purpose of rounds, and protocols for helping host schools develop a focus and follow-up for a day of rounds. But even all of this doesn't fully explain how difficult it is to shift a school system's culture from one that sometimes spends too much time focusing on the deficits of children to one that focuses on the learning of everyone. That won't happen unless we understand the broader organizational problems that the rounds process will ultimately reveal. In short, as the system more regularly does all of the things just described in the first part of the book, it puts pressure on all the adults in ways they haven't dealt with before—pressure that reveals three systemic problems that stand in the path to learning. In part 2, we'll turn to these problems of frequency, symmetry, and reciprocity.

# Solving Problems of Organizational Learning

Large-scale instructional improvement is a complex and counter-cultural task. To understand the use of instructional rounds in service of instructional improvement, one must understand not only the process and protocols of rounds, but also the organizational culture in which that process is used and the systemic problems that tend to arise in large school systems. In this section, we learn how educators actually begin to address these problems. Along the way, we'll return to a question that is at the heart of Lakeside's struggles: *How does a school system reorganize for adult learning, when that learning conflicts with how it has previously done business?*

Suppose that Sofia and other Lakeside educators had the time to step back from their rounds work to think more holistically. In doing so, they might view rounds as something that activates other questions about the school system. We've heard some of these questions already: Why are we doing rounds? What instructional problems are we solving? What's our theory of action? But there are more fundamental ones as well: Is rounds supposed to change the way we interact with one another *in between* rounds visits? Is rounds a model for the kinds of learning that we expect of students? What do we do if some educators *don't want to learn this way*? In part 2 of this book, we'll examine these questions and some preliminary responses to the problems of organizational learning.

## CHAPTER 5

# Finding Time to Practice

## The Problem of Frequency

*The difference between a beginner and a master—*
*is that the master practices a whole lot more.*

*—Yehudi Menuhin*

Rounds requires practice. Lots of practice. Although this might seem like an obvious point, to the Lakeside educators in the midst of busy workdays, practice is sometimes the furthest thing from their minds. There are a number of reasons why an educator might not be willing or able to make time for this practice: as we've seen, some educators are initially unclear what they are making time for, and others aren't convinced at first that rounds is worth their time. The more common reason, however, is that most high school schedules simply do not provide large blocks of time for educators to regularly observe and debrief together during the instructional day. One of the main challenges for Sofia and her colleagues as they try to facilitate the work across Lakeside Public Schools is precisely this problem. In this chapter, we'll look at some initial solutions and their implications.

Sofia is currently the only rounds facilitator, working for the only office that supports all thirty-eight high schools. What this means is that Sofia and her few colleagues in that office currently have the capacity to schedule an official rounds visit with each of the thirty-eight high schools just *once* during the academic year. This also means that school-based staff who are limited in their participation to the district-scheduled rounds visit typically do not get much practice. Given the design of the network, the principals participate in rounds three times a year, but most school staff do not get an opportunity to regularly observe classroom instruction and debrief using the protocols. This fact is important because Sofia has explained that the district wants to "seed" rounds in each of the high schools.

Some of the leaders in Lakeside wonder how often people should practice rounds, because the frequency of the practice sends messages to educators about the nature and kind of learning the district wants to do. If the worries of Sofia and her colleagues are accurate, doing rounds a couple of times a year is like working out at the gym every now and then—one shouldn't expect any lasting results if one doesn't make the gym a habit. In particular, Sofia also worries that doing rounds once a year in a school may even send some counterproductive messages to the educators in the organization: that rounds is an "event" the school does only when the district says it should do so.

Regular, sustained teamwork like rounds is difficult to design in the busy schedules of most high schools. As a result, Lakeside is faced with a problem of frequency: how do we make time and space for educators to regularly learn together in groups for rounds? In this chapter, we'll look at two preliminary solutions that Lakeside is testing. The first tentative solution was intentionally designed by Sofia, Karen, and others in the district office. They've decided to address this problem in part by creating a biweekly, graduate-level professional development "rigor course" for principals and teacher-leaders after school, where part of the curriculum is to practice rounds together. The other solution is emerging concurrently but separately in many of the high schools—educators are using a school-based practice of rounds adapted from the system's rounds practice. We'll look at some of the general ways the high schools are adapting the rounds protocols across the system to use them within the constraints of their busy schedules. Taken together, these two responses will demonstrate that rounds makes educators in the Lakeside system rethink the arrangements of their workday and their patterns for interacting with one another. We'll examine some of the implications of that as well.

## THE "RIGOR COURSE"

It's not unusual for Lakeside to offer professional development and training to teachers. It is also not unusual for Sofia and her colleagues in the Lakeside Public

Schools Central Office to deliver that professional development. It's not surprising then that they would offer professional development to educators about instructional rounds. But what is different about the training they've decided to offer concurrently with instructional rounds is the objectives of this effort. In the past, the district typically provided professional development around particular teaching strategies or programs. For example, many teachers in the district were trained in Readers and Writers Workshop sometime in the past. The program was popular with educators in the district, but has since faded from many schools.

In contrast, the recent objectives of the professional development coming from the district office that supports high schools are quite different. At the end of the first year of instructional rounds, the objectives are now more closely connected to the broader instructional rounds effort happening in the district. These objectives are twofold: (1) to provide additional time and practice for educators from across the system to learn to identify instructional problems, and (2) to provide content and processes that increases educators' capacity for solving those problems collectively. In short, rather than teach specific instructional strategies or programs, the focus has shifted to the relationship between instructional rounds and the system's interest in a common definition of rigor in the classroom. In the course objectives for Lakeside's new rigor course, the syllabus explains this focus:

> **Principals and Teacher-Leaders will:**
> - Learn how to effectively collect, analyze, and utilize student assessments/work and classroom data (instructional rounds) to advance student achievement.
> - Gain practice in facilitating an inquiry community that engages in a continuous cycle of inquiry utilizing new knowledge of student learning around identified instructional problems and measuring progress.
> - Grow in their capacity to share inquiry processes and findings with colleagues.

In contrast to other professional development the district had offered in the past, the purpose of this course was to offer educators a number of processes (of which instructional rounds was one) that might help them observe and understand what is happening in the classrooms in their schools, rather than teach specific instructional programs or design. Lakeside supported this focus on classroom observations with required readings about the brain, learning, and the use of protocols by teams (see exhibit 5.1, "The Rigor Course").

---

EXHIBIT 5.1

## The Rigor Course

*What follows is an excerpt from the syllabus of Lakeside Public Schools' professional development course. The course met after school, every other week during the academic year. Principals and teacher-leaders from the high schools were eligible to enroll in the course, and received course credit from a local university.*

### Purpose

The working definition of academic rigor in [our schools] is helping students develop the capacity to understand content that is complex, ambiguous, thought-provoking, and personally or emotionally challenging. Rigor can be identified in three areas: *content, instruction, and assessment.* In [our schools], a complete rigorous learning experience must include: *high expectations, high relevance, and appropriate support.* The combination of these three components must be found in every lesson, in every classroom, of every school. Only then will we realize *higher student engagement and learning* across ALL schools.

Improving academic rigor is an articulated goal, but what does "rigor" actually mean? What, exactly, does it look like in the classroom? Does it look the same across content areas? What concrete pedagogical moves will help teachers increase rigor in their classrooms, and what are the perceived risks involved with raising the level of academic task and expectation in the classroom? What supports do teachers need from principals in learning how to increase rigor in their classrooms? In this course, we will come, over time, to an understanding of how quantitative and qualitative information about student learning can be used to make evidence-based decisions that lead to higher student engagement, high-level learning, and growth. The high quality evidence-based decisions that teachers will be able to make will enable them to address the goals and targets from the Superintendent's Agenda.

The key strategy to achieve these goals is to provide powerful, ongoing, embedded and collaborative professional development for identified teacher-leaders to strengthen teaching practice and distributive leadership across schools and district.

### Course Content and Design

Teacher-leaders from high schools will explore this concept of academic rigor and lead a cycle of inquiry. Simultaneously, principals will be engaged in like inquiry in high school district Professional Learning Sessions to foster a sense of school and district cohesion. Participants will attend and support three district instructional rounds for cross-school learning. Leading for Rigorous Instructional Decision Making will include a series of seminars, online sessions, triad instructional rounds, one departmental instructional round, and over-the-shoulder coaching. Embedded in the inquiry will be a focus on Information Decision Progress processes and protocols to use for effective facilitating. The ultimate goal of the inquiry is to bring to scale a common understanding of academic rigor as well as to establish sound research practices across all high schools.

**Course Requirements**

1. *Course Binder*

Binders will include:

- Agendas and minutes from team meetings.

- Summaries of findings from student assessment/student work analysis that demonstrates new understanding of academic rigor and the inquiry approach.

- Findings from work with a case-study student and documentation of progress toward academic learning targets.

- Summary of findings from instructional rounds that demonstrate new understandings of academic rigor.

- Team action plan based on student assessments, instructional rounds, and inquiry with next steps that demonstrate new understanding of academic rigor.

2. *Reflections*

Participants will write six reflections based on readings, observations of classroom practice, and work with teams. These reflections will include a description of their reading or observation process, initial understandings, questions and responses, and content/outcomes of team discussions. All reflections should be word processed and double-spaced. Citations should follow appropriate APA or MIA formatting. Reflections will be evaluated on the basis of presentation, content, analysis, self-reflection and critique, development of ideas, and overall cohesion.

3. *Observation of Team Facilitation*

Each participant will be observed at least one time in the spring. Participants will receive over-the-shoulder coaching and feedback on their facilitative practice and process.

*continued*

4. *Case-Study Student Expo*

Each participant will participate in case-study student expo, which will involve synthesizing course learning into a 10-minute small group presentation.

5. *Culminating Class Product*

Course participants will collaborate to design a rigorous instructional practices rubric.

**Required Readings**

Lorin W. Anderson and David R. Krathwohl, eds., *A Taxonomy for Learning, Teaching, and Assessing: A Revision of Bloom's Taxonomy of Educational Objectives*, abridged ed. (New York: Longman, 2001).

John D. Bransford, Ann L. Brown, and Rodney R. Cocking, eds., Committee on Developments in the Science of Learning, *How People Learn: Brain, Mind, Experience, and School* (Washington, DC: National Academy Press, 1999).

Elizabeth A. City et al., *Instructional Rounds in Education: A Network Approach to Improving Teaching and Learning* (Cambridge, MA: Harvard Education Press, 2009).

Ruth Hubbard and Brenda Power, *Living the Questions: A Guide for Teacher-Researchers* (York, ME: Stenhouse, 1999).

Joseph P. McDonald et al., *The Power of Protocols: An Educator's Guide to Better Practice* (New York: Teachers College Press, 2007).

W. James Popham, *Classroom Assessment: What Teachers Need to Know*, 6th ed. (Upper Saddle River, NJ: Prentice Hall, 2010).

Robert J. Sternberg, "Excellence for All," *Educational Leadership* 66 (October 2008): 14–19.

Carol Ann Tomlinson. *How to Differentiate Instruction in Mixed-Ability Classrooms*, 2nd ed. (Alexandria, VA: Association for Supervision and Curriculum Development, 2001).

Tony Wagner, "Rigor Redefined," *Educational Leadership* 66 (October 2008): 20–25.

There were several reasons why principals and teacher-leaders might take this course, including graduate-level credit and an interest in instructional rounds. Whatever the reason, all of the thirty-five educators who enrolled in the first rigor course were also required to help facilitate instructional rounds in their school, meaning that each would take on a leadership role associated with Lakeside's improvement process. This feature of the course was an important part of Lakeside's interest in having all the high schools use rounds on their own and increasing the frequency of contact that educators had with the process and with each other. The course syllabus explains some of these requirements and outcomes:

- Teacher-leaders will be able to guide their departments in an ongoing cycle of inquiry that includes instructional rounds, analysis of student assessments/work samples, as well as identification of next steps.
- Teacher-leaders will know how to effectively communicate what they have learned in academic rigor seminars to help identify instructional problems and possible next steps for their department.
- Teacher-leaders will be able to facilitate departmental instructional rounds and [will know] how to use findings to identify possible next steps for their school and department.

These objectives put many of the teacher-leaders in a position to effectively communicate the purpose and practice of rounds to the other teachers in their school, which also made them an important asset to their principals.

The course was not without its problems, as Sofia and her colleagues would attest. In fact, it was very much under design as they taught it that first year, particularly as Sofia and her colleagues learned more about how people were using rounds during the district-sponsored rounds visits each week. But the course was cotaught by several departments within the district office, and this forced different administrators to think about how their work connected to one another and how they would communicate those connections to the educators enrolled in the class. In this way, the learning for Sofia and her colleagues was as important as the learning for the educators enrolled in the course. One of Sofia's coteachers explained this phenomenon: "I think that all the work [teaching] together has really been, in large part, about fostering mutual understanding. You know, so it has been very helpful to hear how Sofia talks about rounds and to observe [her]conducting instructional rounds and for her to hear [me] talk about [another improvement process] and just to have conversations among the team about what this could look like."

The rigor course took several steps toward addressing this problem of frequency. First, it increased both the number of educators practicing rounds in the district, as well as the frequency of that practice. Teachers in the course were able to practice the rounds process using videos of classroom instruction, debrief with their classmates using the rounds protocol, and get real-time feedback from Sofia and her colleagues about how they were doing. Second, the teachers enrolled in the course got an opportunity to help lead a district-sponsored rounds day at their school during the year. They immediately became an asset to their principals and an important member of the rounds network more broadly. The rigor course also increased the frequency and depth of the interaction between the district office staff who cotaught the course. In planning and delivering the instruction for the rigor course, they regularly had to meet with one another to talk about the purpose and practice of instructional rounds.

## SCHOOL-BASED ROUNDS

Throughout this book, we've seen that instructional rounds in the Lakeside school system rests on a particular view of improvement—one where educators are increasingly given control over their own learning within the rounds protocols. (Only the network of principals was initially required to participate in rounds, but Lakeside left it up to them how they might include their instructional staff over time. The rigor course was also an optional feature for classroom educators.) One expression of this gradual release of control from the system to the educators is the school-based practice of instructional rounds happening in between Lakeside's official rounds visits.

Of the thirty-eight high school principals, many are now beginning to think about other ways to involve their instructional staff in rounds. The principals typically say they are learning a great deal about rounds through their monthly professional development sessions, the rigor course, or the district-sponsored rounds visits. But most of their instructional staff aren't regularly exposed to the protocols or the discussions about teaching and learning—exposure that the network of principals enjoyed. Some of this is a result of the design of the network. Because Sofia and Karen intentionally started with principals, the relatively infrequent practice of rounds by the instructional staff is one trade-off of this design. However, Sofia and many of the principals increasingly see value in making the rounds practice a more frequent feature of each high school, but they wonder, how do they do rounds regularly within the busy schedules of a high school?

### Getting Started

To answer this question, let's begin by examining how some principals think about involving their instructional staff in rounds. Soon after attending a visit or hosting rounds at their own school, many Lakeside principals saw a reason to begin developing their own plans for introducing rounds to their instructional staff. As one principal named Margaret explained to me, her goal that year was "to get every teacher who wants it to get some experience with rounds." This was an ambitious goal, but she was also worried about how it might be received by her school: "My first step was to get my [assistants and department heads] to understand it and to try it. We did it by having them read the first five chapters of the book [*Instructional Rounds*] to see what they thought there. I didn't coerce them into this is the right or wrong way; I just presented it as, 'What do you think of this?'"

Like other Lakeside principals, she needed to find out how much support there might be within the school for rounds before introducing it to the entire instructional staff. She asked her assistants and department heads to practice rounds a couple of times with her, and then they discussed it: "And then, once they tried it, it was their first evidence that there is a pattern [across classrooms]. It was kind of interesting how some of the administrators were a little bit shocked—they were making a connection between the way teachers were teaching and the critical-thinking skills the students were using. But they thought it was great to see different teachers that they would normally not see. So, they saw people they were supervising and others they weren't."

After testing the waters with their leadership teams, many principals began to reach out more broadly to the instructional staff in their schools to invite them to participate in rounds. Several of these principals asked for volunteers who wanted to give up their planning period a few times a quarter to practice rounds. A typical process looked like this: first, the principals would survey the instructional staff in their buildings to see how many might be interested in participating and which teachers would also be willing to have their classrooms visited by observers. Some teachers wanted to observe, others were willing to open their doors to observation teams, some were interested in doing both, and some initially wanted no part of the process. Exhibit 5.2, "The Problem of Frequency: How Leaders Can Adapt Instructional Rounds for School-Based Practice," describes a general process used by principals in Lakeside for introducing rounds to instructional staff.

---

**EXHIBIT 5.2**

### The Problem of Frequency: How Leaders Can Adapt
### Instructional Rounds for School-Based Practice

*What follows is a process and staffing plan used by some Lakeside Public Schools principals for scheduling teachers into observation groups for a school-based version of rounds. Teachers volunteered their planning periods several times a semester in order to free up time without requiring substitute teachers. This plan requires that the rounds teams meet after school and sometimes several days after the classroom observations. This is a trade-off that the principals have to weigh. Adaptation of rounds in this way is likely to create more opportunities for people to practice observing in teams, although it loses some of the freshness of the data for the debrief.*

**Gather Information on Teachers' Interest in Participating**

1. Survey teachers for interest in doing classroom observations during their planning period.

2. At the same time, survey teachers for those willing to host teams of observers. Many Lakeside principals had teachers indicate which periods they were willing to have visitors, and which they would prefer not to have observers. Some teachers decided they would prefer not to participate at all.

**Make an Observation Schedule**

3. Group teachers who are interested in observing and who share the same planning period. In this case, sharing a grade or content area is not as important as finding groups of teachers who are willing and available to observe instruction at the same time.

4. Schedule each of those observation teams for two 20-minute observations during a shared planning period on one day of a week. This will take some careful planning to determine which classroom teachers are willing to host the observers at that time.

**Schedule the Debrief**

5. Because the classroom observations will take place during educators' 50-minute planning period, there isn't time to debrief immediately after

observing. Many Lakeside principals are asking teams that observed during the week to debrief together after school or at the end of the week. Some principals let educators credit this time toward other professional development requirements, or allowed them to opt out of other duties if they regularly meet for rounds.

Principals would often ask the instructional staff who were interested to practice with them first. The group of interested educators would first observe generic classroom videos at one of their regular staff meetings and practice the rounds protocols before anyone was turned loose for rounds in the school. Margaret explained the process of introducing it to the instructional staff:

> I framed it initially as gathering data so that we can inform our professional development. In simplest terms. But once we had, you know, a couple two or three rounds of data gathering, we definitely saw patterns, and it helped us define more clearly our problem of practice. So, then I continued to say to the staff, "Yes, this helps inform our professional development, but also helps us learn where we have grown and where we still need to grow in terms of learning for our students." Sometimes teachers will push back and say, "How do you know that [a lack of rigor] is a problem? Why are you saying this is a problem?" I said, "Well, this is what it's been in the past, but there's no guarantee it continues to be a problem." That's why we're going to continue doing instructional rounds.

## Adapting the Rounds Protocols

As already mentioned, the successful practice of rounds requires lots of practice with strong, consistent protocols for observing and debriefing classroom observation data. However, there is no evidence that that these protocols need to be implemented exactly the same way in every school to be useful or effective. In my own experience, some elements of rounds are nonnegotiable. One common saying about rounds reinforces this idea: "Observation before description, description before analysis, analysis before prediction, prediction before prescription." In other words, the core practice of conducting nonjudgmental classroom observations in teams has a logical sequence, which allows us to have evidence-based discussions about classroom data that will be useful to a host site (or a group of classrooms) and will contribute to the learning of the observers. At the same time, there's nothing to suggest that rounds requires a school to make the same number of classroom visits each time or that there is an ideal amount of time in which this process should occur. In fact, the amount of time a team or network requires to do a cycle of rounds most likely depends a great deal on how much experience the participants have with the protocols.

Nonetheless, a major problem is indeed finding time in the day for observation and discussion of the data. The most common way the Lakeside principals addressed this problem was by leveraging teachers' planning period a couple times a year. Most of the teachers' planning periods are 50 minutes long, which leaves just enough time for them to participate in two 20-minute classroom observations. However, this period provides virtually no time to debrief the data. Since only a fraction of the teaching staff of any school typically shares a planning period, most Lakeside principals wondered how they would make time for the observation teams to debrief together after observing in classrooms. In response, several principals began to adapt and adjust the timing of the protocols to fit within the particular school schedules of their instructional staff (see exhibit 5.2, "The Problem of Frequency: How Leaders Can Adapt Instructional Rounds for School-Based Practice," for details). Thus, educators would often complete the debrief after school on the day of their classroom observations. Other principals planned an after-school meeting on the Friday of the week that teachers would be observing instruction, and had the teams go though the debrief together that afternoon. In either case, these adaptations meant that the data wasn't as fresh in the minds of the observers, but it did create some flexibility that allowed teachers to observe together more often, without the school's having to hire substitute teachers or wait for the district to come once a year. Moreover, these after-school debriefs gave the teams enough time to go through the entire rounds protocol together. Margaret explained that the response has been mostly positive to this kind of adaptation so far. Lately, the educators have been observing for, and learning about, higher-order thinking, and they are starting to get some agreement on the need for this in their classrooms:

> I get varied responses. Some teachers, they think it's very obvious that as a school we need to move toward more active learning so our students have more opportunities to engage in higher-order thinking. They're very against the chalk and talk . . . Some teachers, they're newer teachers to teaching, but not always. And, then I have a contingent of teachers where this information is very shocking and new. Not [that] they're completely against it; it's just a surprising revelation when they have to make

a connection between how they are teaching and what kind of critical-thinking skills students are using. And so I've had mixed responses. I think sometimes the teachers who understand get very impatient with those who don't. And I've had a lot of it in smaller groups of teachers, so no more than twenty teachers at a time, and I always try to make sure I have someone who has done instructional rounds before there, because they're usually a great support in terms of explaining it or giving the teachers perspectives on why this will help build our school in the right direction.

By the end of the year, nearly every teacher in this school had voluntarily participated in two 20-minute periods of observation and an afternoon debrief. In my last conversation with Margaret, she indicated that next year's school schedule will automatically build the observation time and debrief into the school's staffing schedule. This suggests that the rounds process has become a permanent fixture in the professional life of this school.

## THE PROBLEM OF FREQUENCY: SOME LESSONS

Let's return to the problem Sofia and her colleagues posed at the beginning of this chapter. Initially, one of the puzzling features about rounds is purely a technical problem of time—in short, how to make time for all this group work. One important lesson is that what you make time for depends largely on your purpose for rounds. In the first year, Lakeside wanted to use rounds to create a process for principals to begin generating some common understanding of the instructional problems their schools shared and what rigorous classrooms might look and sound like. Thus, most of the people learning and using rounds were limited to the principals' rounds network that first year. However, both Sofia and some of the principals worried that not giving instructional staff access to that information might send some problematic messages by the beginning of the second year of rounds.

One way the central office dealt with this problem was by changing the focus of professional development opportunities for instructional staff in the system. Professional development in this school system now provides instructional staff a regular opportunity to learn the purpose and practice of rounds. Educators and professional development providers have frequent contact with the rounds observation protocols as part of that professional development. In addition, the rigor course is also an incubator for teacher-leaders to serve as rounds facilitators.

In the meantime, principals are starting to adapt the rounds protocols to increase the practice's availability to instructional staff. Because the schools couldn't always afford to pay for substitute teachers every time teachers wanted to practice rounds, they made some adjustments so that teachers could observe during planning periods and debrief after school. It's probably too early to assess the impact of all these in-school rounds processes both on the school and on the overall system. In fact, Sofia and the principals' network will likely have to be vigilant in protecting the descriptive, nonjudgmental approach that Sofia teaches so that rounds is not used for supervision or evaluation in any school. In addition, the relationship between in-school rounds and district-sponsored rounds will probably need to be articulated to preserve a coherent message to educators.

These examples also raise several questions. The most important question is whether adapting the instructional rounds protocols will affect how educators learn about instruction. For example, how should schools and principals think about the trade-off between creating time for teams to observe more frequently and having the debrief immediately following observations? Second, how might the school system be affected if thirty-eight high schools adapt the rounds process in different ways? Sofia wants to gradually transfer control of this process to the high schools, which will likely result in some variation in how people practice rounds. It's hard to predict what the result of that variation might be.

This last issue is related to one discussed at the beginning of the chapter—that having a coherent, long-term strategy will help prevent rounds from devolving to the point that thirty-eight high schools are doing their own thing. Neither a focus on rigor nor instructional rounds by itself is an improvement strategy—at least not in the sense that Sofia is ultimately planning and hoping for. That is, a shift to adult learning probably means thinking more carefully about how these different efforts relate to one another. Therefore, Lakeside will likely have to continue to articulate the relationship between the principals' network, school-based rounds, and the rigor course. If Lakeside can better convey how the various adult learning programs interrelate in the long term, then the high schools' use of these programs may contribute to the larger system's goals.

Finally, doing rounds in Lakeside has resulted in at least two disruptions to the typical ways educators work with one another. First, the practice of rounds has formally shifted the focus and objectives of professional development in the form of the rigor course. Second, it has made principals and teachers reallocate time within the daily schedule for the purpose of observation and discussion of instructional practice. These shifts in how educators allocate their work time are closely linked to the frequency of rounds. The more that people practice rounds, the more they question how they spend their professional time. The more they question how they spend their professional time, the greater their imagination for finding time for a practice like rounds. In other words, educators don't tend to question the rules or patterns for how they do their work unless they're asked to practice differently. At the same time, they don't practice differently unless they have a reason to question the rules or patterns for how they have typically done their work.

Although this is a fairly complicated issue, the problem of frequency primarily has technical solutions that seem doable almost anywhere that educators are interested in finding time to observe and talk about their instructional practice. That's not to say that these technical problems are easy to solve. But in contrast to the cultural problems of schools we'll look at in chapters 6 and 7, the technical problems of frequency pale in comparison. One of these mostly cultural problems—symmetry—is the subject of the next chapter.

## CHAPTER 6

# Modeling Learning
## The Problem of Symmetry

*Academic rigor can be defined as the goal of helping students
develop the capacity to understand content that is complex, ambiguous,
thought-provoking, and personally or emotionally challenging.*

—*Lakeside Public Schools principals, "A Statement on Rigor"*

**"A**mbiguous," "thought-provoking," "emotionally challenging"—Lakeside's statement on rigor is full of terms that are up for debate and potentially controversial, depending on one's views about the kinds of learning kids should do in schools. Stepping into classrooms in Lakeside reveals a huge range of ideas about how kids learn and what sort of tasks or classroom arrangements result in learning. These ideas represent lots of potential examples of what adults and kids might do in a rigorous classroom. As we saw in part 1, the principals don't yet agree on the issue of instructional rigor; nor do the educators responsible for that instruction. Of course, one of the purposes of instructional rounds in Lakeside is to help generate some common ideas and understanding about rigor.

In these respects, Lakeside is a completely normal school district. One of the consistent features of instruction in American schools is that it *is* so highly variable (much more variable, in fact, than in most other developed countries). Most school reform ideas in the United States attack this variability in one of two ways. The first way is by coming down hard on how teachers teach, usually by scripting both the curriculum and specific teacher moves down to the minute. The other way is by articulating very specific measures of what constitutes success (and coming down hard on failure) under the assumption that educators will figure out what to do if systems or state education departments demonstrate how serious they are about improvement. Currently, this is the accountability system under which most American states and localities, including Lakeside Public Schools, are operating.

Instructional rounds is an exception to these two dominant school reform approaches (or, in the case of the current accountability system, in spite of them). We've already outlined how instructional rounds diverges from more typical school reform programs by focusing on observation of instruction, networks, and theories of action. We've also identified how articulating a problem of practice allows educators to take control of their own learning in ways that differ from other school reform programs. But the regular practice in Lakeside is surfacing a more general problem that separates rounds further from typical school reform ideas: *instructional rounds is a pretty good model for the kinds of rigor that Lakeside wants its students to experience, but these qualities are the very ones that sometimes make educators initially dislike instructional rounds.* We'll examine the problem in this chapter.

In my conversations with Lakeside principals, district staff, and teachers, nearly all express a desire to see Lakeside students complete more rigorous school work. By rigorous, they usually mean school tasks where students have conversations with one another, using academic language, and produce individual or group products that show command of that academic language and an understanding of how different concepts relate to one another. Some of the educators I spoke with said they know how to design these kinds of lessons. Some of them said they assigned such lessons regularly. All of them had personal theories for why this sort of work doesn't (or can't) happen more regularly in high schools.

In many ways, rounds is exactly the kind of rigorous task that many educators wish their students were able to do more frequently. It is a cognitively demanding group process that requires high levels of sustained effort and an understanding of how different instructional concepts might be related to one another. Educators practicing rounds regularly have to analyze observation data, predict what students are learning, and often defend their own ideas in order to feel that they are successfully participating during instructional rounds. They also have to learn to use new, specialized language and norms of discourse, just as students learning academic discourse must do. However, many of the educators I spoke with initially disliked rounds for the very reasons that make it a rigorous task: some of the work is ambiguous, and it is often emotionally challenging. This work is ambiguous because high-level tasks like rounds have many routes to arrive at an answer; it's emotionally challenging because the work is intellectually difficult and requires educators to examine one another's assumptions and beliefs about instruction.

Thus, symmetry is both a technical and a cultural problem. A symmetrical school or school system is one that expects educators and students at all levels of the organization to do similar kinds of learning, regardless of role, title, or positional authority. Therefore, the problem of symmetry raises questions such as these: "What can rounds tell us about the relationship between adult and student learning?" "Should the learning we do as adults model the type of learning that we expect of students?" "And if so, what should that look like?" School reformers sometimes write about symmetry in the context of fixing school accountability systems.[1] In general, some suggest that more powerful systems would share accountability across all levels of the system: student, teacher, administrator, district office, state office. In other words, everyone at all levels would share responsibility for student performance.

Symmetry in accountability seems promising, but let's take it a step further. What if everyone in a school system had the same general requirements for demonstrating *learning*? In other words, what if everyone in the system shared responsibility for learning and modeling that learning? In the Lakeside example, instructional rounds generally requires educators to do the kinds of cognitively demanding work that they wish their students would do. Thus, rounds is a step toward a more symmetrical organization. But why is a more symmetrical organization a good thing? Relatively symmetrical organizations tend to favor networks over hierarchy, observation of practice over evaluation, and theories of action rather than premature solutions. These conditions are the same ones that rounds needs in order to be effective—in other words, the properties of a symmetrical organization and the practice of rounds are inextricably linked to one another in the long term.

In a more immediate way, regularly participating in instructional rounds can help educators understand what it's like for students to struggle with rigorous or cognitively demanding tasks. This is why describing and understanding the problem of symmetry is so important. However, symmetry does not come easily and is difficult to understand unless you have experienced it. To make this idea more concrete, we'll look at what happens when educators—who in this case are trying to create more rigorous classrooms for students—are confronted with rigorous tasks of their own during rounds, learning alongside their colleagues, and occasionally resisting the whole process.

## STRUGGLING WITH AMBIGUITY

For the purposes of this book, the key question about symmetry is whether the regular practice of instructional rounds might help Lakeside educators understand how their students experience rigorous tasks and how that might someday lead to different instruction. Since they're using rounds to help develop some common understanding about rigor, we'll use Lakeside's concepts of *ambiguity* and *emotionally challenging* as two ways to talk about rigorous classroom tasks. This doesn't mean that the principals' definition is the only way to talk about tasks, but their version of rigor has captured two important elements of what we'll call *high-level tasks.*

There's a fair amount of evidence that high-level tasks (for readers familiar with Bloom's Taxonomy, I'm referring to classroom work that falls in the upper half of the domains: *analyzing, evaluating, creating*) share several common characteristics. First, high-level tasks tend to allow different routes to a solution. For example, a high school student who is asked to *evaluate* the impact of a new oil and gas pipeline installed across three Midwestern states could do so in terms of the economic impact of the new jobs created by construction crews. Or the student might evaluate the environmental impact of the above-ground pipe on migrating herds of prairie animals. A teacher could also ask a group of students to *create* a map of alternate paths for the oil and gas pipeline—paths that minimize the environmental impact while maximizing potential economic benefits. In this case, the students would have to negotiate their own beliefs and knowledge with others in the group to complete the task. Clearly, one can imagine any number of potential solutions that might meet the requirements of these assignments at the high school level, suggesting some level of ambiguity in the task. In contrast, a task that only requires a student to *remember* (a relatively low-level task of memorization) a set of environmental laws or economic principles by matching the terms to the correct definition might not allow students to struggle with a complexity of issues involved in the scenario like the one just described. There is less ambiguity in this last example.

The goal of the task is quite clear in all three examples, but the tasks can have different levels of ambiguity depending on the options, choices, or complexities that a student is given. We know that Lakeside thinks rigorous tasks are based in part on ambiguity. As we've seen, ambiguity means allowing for multiple routes to a correct answer. But, given our interest in symmetry, how do adults experience these kinds of tasks?

As an adult group task, instructional rounds is inherently ambiguous because there are many potential routes for the group to address a problem of practice. While the protocols help make the goal and boundaries of the task clear, there's a great deal of ambiguity at several points in the process. Let's look at some of this ambiguity.

One of the most common sources of ambiguity is in the creation and use of categories and labels for patterns of the observation data. In part 1, we saw examples of how groups of educators might organize and label their observation data in looking for patterns of instruction across classrooms. In these examples, the educators argued and questioned one another about the names for these categories. There was a good deal of discussion about what each term actually meant and which types of data might fall into each category. For example, they argued about whether a task might exist in more than one category at one time. Some educators questioned whether their chart was accurate or whether some other arrangement might better represent the learning they saw in the classroom. Clearly, there is more than one way to think about a problem of practice, and this ambiguity is similar to the types of rigorous tasks that Lakeside wants it students to experience.

## THE EMOTIONAL CHALLENGES OF HIGH-LEVEL TASKS

Because of this ambiguity, high-level tasks tend to share another important characteristic. These kinds of tasks often elicit stronger emotional responses from learners as a result of their complexity and because they often require perseverance in the face of conflicting information, disagreements, and even feelings of failure. In the examples of the oil and gas pipeline lesson, it might be tempting for a teacher to end the unit once the students memorized the environmental laws and economic principles that govern the placement of the pipeline, rather than trying the more ambiguous, higher-level tasks. In reality, the pipeline scenario is quite complicated, activating a series of perplexing political and value-based considerations, as well as economic and environmental factors. But it's often difficult for a teacher to know how to manage and guide students through this range of issues, particularly if students might not know how to have these kinds of conversations with one another. At the same time, students gain evaluative skills when they struggle with these questions and with one another, even if the students don't necessarily enjoy all parts of that work.

Similarly, Sofia might feel the urge to provide educators with the names, definitions, and categories for organizing observation data during instructional rounds.

As we've seen, these patterns are quite important, and she might be tempted to give the educators specific guidance on what to look for in the classroom or how to organize this data during the debrief. But that would simplify the task in ways that would undermine the learning she wants them all to do. Instead, Sofia lets groups of educators struggle with the ambiguous parts of the practice, even as they tend to get frustrated with this process and with one another. We saw some of this frustration in one exchange in chapter 2 as a group of educators tried to organize their observation data:

"I'm not sure we did this right," remarked one educator.

Sofia suggested that "there's no right way to organize the data."

Several minutes later, the educator again looked to Sofia to affirm that they were on the correct path.

"Yeah, but the sticky note I wrote is wrong, right?" the educator asked.

Sofia explained, "You can always take it down or change it if you have other evidence you want to include."

"Oh. OK. I feel better. This is stressful."

Most often, the resistance to the ambiguous parts of rounds would manifest itself in feelings of confusion about what the "right" answer might be. Other times, a member of the network might stop participating out of frustration—instead, the person might spend time checking his or her cell phone or getting up often to look at what other groups were doing. In other cases, an educator might leave the room altogether and return several minutes later. In one case, I watched an educator leave the group and not return for the rest of the day.

In any event, participating in instructional rounds can clearly be emotionally challenging as educators deal with the ambiguous parts of the tasks. But rather than shy away from the practice for this reason, Lakeside could use this challenge as a point of learning for everyone in the network. It's difficult for leaders or rounds facilitators to know exactly how to manage these dynamics every time they arise, but here are a couple of tips:

- Don't feel compelled to provide answers during rounds just because some educators are struggling with the process. In fact, you should model and talk about your own struggles when they arise.
- Save time at the end of rounds to talk with the network members about what it's like to struggle in groups with one another.
- Take time to name the characteristic of rounds that might make it a high-level or rigorous task (or whatever language is appropriate in your context).

- Brainstorm how students might feel in doing the same kinds of rigorous tasks.
- With practice, these discussions can form the basis for thinking about how adults can model the types of learning they might want for students.

These examples of high-level student and adult tasks, at first glance so different from one another, illustrate this problem of symmetry quite well. Both adults and students find the tasks ambiguous and emotionally challenging, and these are strong indicators of learning in both cases. More importantly, Lakeside educators practicing instructional rounds are likely to learn something about how their students experience rigorous tasks, which is a step toward understanding and managing the problem of symmetry.

Because how educators talk about and understand these issues across Lakeside exceeds the importance of any particular solution to the problem, I decided to ask Lakeside educators if there were parts of the process they found difficult or frustrating. I thought this might help Sofia and her colleagues understand what aspects of instructional rounds—as a high-level task—might help educators learn about rigorous instruction. The educators mentioned a number of issues. Importantly, they say they are learning something, but they also have questions and frustrations that tell us something about rounds as a high-level task. What's more, not every difficulty or confusion associated with instructional rounds is necessarily a sign of learning. But Sofia's careful use of protocols and the various ways she supports learning make it more likely that the stories quoted below are a productive form of learning.

One educator named Carrie shared with me her frustrations about what happens when each observation group offers suggestions to the host school at the end of the day—during the next level of work. One of the small groups on this particular day suggested that the host school consider "releasing responsibility" more often to students in the classroom. Carrie explained:

> The [recommendation] about releasing responsibility . . . I think it would be kind of hard to just sort of get that information and then be like, "OK. So, you know, what does that mean? What are they talking about specifically? What would that look like?" I think if a second- or third-year teacher were getting that kind of feedback, it would probably be really helpful if the person who wrote the feedback also had an extra, I don't know, three hours in which they could sit down first of all and explain what they were talking about. Maybe come up with a plan with that teacher as to how to do that. Then, maybe come back for another observation and maybe come

back again after all that had happened and say, "Hey, do you think it was better? Have I improved? Have I not?"

Carrie worried about how the adults on the receiving end of the recommendations from a day of instructional rounds might feel. Specifically, she wondered if a second- or third-year teacher would know what it means for a teacher to "release responsibility" to students and how or when a teacher should do that. She worried that the participants had left the host school with some unusable information. In response to this worry, she described a hypothetical process where the observation teams sit down with teachers to explain the patterns and recommendations. This idea also reflected her interest in getting the recommendations right the first time because she wasn't sure when she might have an opportunity to meet with these folks again. In other words, the frequency of rounds probably has an impact on how people both deliver and receive the data, a tension that this educator described nicely for us here. Of course, these are also the challenges of trying to make learning a requirement of everyone in the system, especially when that learning is extremely complex and done at scale.

Jeff worried about the learning that happens after the visiting observation teams leave:

> I'm wondering what the follow-up is. I'm wondering where this goes from here. So, I know that the school is expected to identify the next level of work. I know that . . . some of these schools have developed action steps that they're excited about carrying forward and some schools . . . it seems like the school had some steps they were excited about but also some frustration about not having a very high degree of specificity about what to do next. And I'm just kind of wondering where [there will be] the next conversation with the school about what they tried on as a result of instructional rounds and whether or not that made any difference and how do they know it made a difference.

Perhaps no comment better illustrates the complexity and ambiguity of the tasks inherent in instructional rounds than the idea that the participants might not have "a very high degree of specificity about what to do next." Of course, this is a common feeling when anyone attempts to solve a complicated problem, but one the school system wants its students to experience as well. During instructional rounds, the educators are experiencing what it feels like to work on rigorous group tasks, and this seems like useful learning for the system if it makes educators more likely to understand how students experience these tasks. Certainly, the network could do some very specific things to help a host school with the follow-up to a network visit, but part of the learning is developing those processes and expectations over time.

As people gain more experience with instructional rounds, there are a range of other issues that affect the learning of the network. Stephanie, a principal, has practiced rounds regularly, but now has to be patient while other educators learn what to do: "I guess at the beginning we spent a lot of time explaining what rounds is and what its purpose is, and that would take at least an hour if not more. For me, I just want to jump in doing it. And I think one thing that could probably make it more effective is . . . [if] maybe those who haven't [had experience with rounds] could get some more information before everyone else arrives in terms of nonjudgmental observations and so on."

Another common characteristic of high-level tasks is that they can typically result in a wide range of completion rates among participants. In a high school classroom, this means that students might be working at different speeds on different parts of an assignment at the same time. As educators learn more, the instructional rounds network has to figure out what to do when adults have different levels of knowledge and experience with the protocols. Specifically, they have to learn how to train and involve new members in the network on a regular basis and how to differentiate their support according to an educator's knowledge and experience. Importantly, this is a problem that classroom teachers must deal with regularly as they support students who are at different stages of development and who might also be new to their classroom.

## MODELING A LEARNING PROCESS FOR ADULTS

Taken together, all of these examples demonstrate that instructional rounds is a powerful example of the sort of learning we might want students to do. But part of the problem of symmetry is both figuring out how to support adults as they experience these kinds of high-level tasks and make these connections to their own teaching clear to them. The most obvious way that the rounds process models this for the adults is through a rounds facilitator's behavior. Although Sofia is a "teacher" of instructional rounds, she also participates with the official learners in the process from start to finish: she too observes and takes notes in the classrooms and participates in the debrief over the morning and into the afternoon. But her role as facilitator typically diminishes throughout the day and weeks, as other educators take on facilitator and teaching roles. In particular, the educators who are enrolled in Sofia's rigor course typically take on facilitation roles early and often during the network visits for which Sofia is responsible. In this way, she also models the gradual release of responsibility from teacher to student, as described earlier. All of these behaviors help to model symmetry for the educators—and Sofia doesn't ask anyone to do anything she isn't willing to do herself.

But there are more subtle ways that the rounds network has begun to model adult learning, and this seems to carry powerful messages to the educators (and students) in Lakeside. One of the most important features of the design of this network is that multiple district-level staff, including the academic and assistant academic superintendent for high schools, the administrators for special education, and departments for English language learners regularly attend rounds each week in the high schools. One can imagine a scenario where these administrators dominated the conversation with their presence and knowledge. Instead, I found that these administrators were much more likely to listen, ask questions, and defer to the school host during the day. And many principals who were accountable to these administrators appreciated how these district staff members participated. In this way, everyone has the same general requirements for learning about instruction, and this too helps to address the problem of symmetry.

Importantly, this feature of the network did not always go smoothly. In particular, the district office had some growing pains as it worked out the attendance requirements for district office staff—they all were responsible for a number of initiatives on any given day, and instructional rounds cut deeply into their time for doing that other work. Sofia and her colleagues in the district office had several difficult conversations about their collective commitments to the work after district staff occasionally had to leave rounds sessions early for other meetings and commitments. She and others were worried about the message it might send when district staff were leaving in the middle of the debrief. In the end, these difficult conversations led to increased understanding and commitment to each other, though the conversation will probably have to be continued as the network grows.

Chris, a teacher, shared a different concern with me about inviting members of the host school to listen to the debrief of the classroom observation data, even though these educators from the host school had not joined in the classroom observations that day: "I don't think there should be a whole-school debrief when a group of outsiders comes in and collaborates with some of the staff there to do one day of rounds when they see a limited portion of limited classes . . . So, I don't think it's a good idea, and I think it can potentially turn teachers off to the whole concept of rounds . . . And I don't think . . . having gone through rounds myself . . . I support doing rounds, and I think there's value in doing rounds, but I don't think that the data and the conclusions they yield from doing one day of rounds is reliable."

Chris's concerns about making "conclusions" based on data from "one day of rounds" is important—if people in the organization see rounds as an event, then they feel far too much pressure to get the data "right," rather than see it as a process they will return to again in the near future. As a result, this educator does not want to share the data with the entire school, because he worries that those staff members won't have enough context and experience with rounds to appreciate the patterns. This is a dilemma that Sofia and her colleagues have been managing throughout the process and will continue to think about. On one hand, they want the educators who were not making classroom observations that day to feel welcome to hear the patterns of instruction during the debrief. On the other hand, those patterns may not make a great deal of sense to those who didn't observe in classrooms or who are unfamiliar with the rounds process. In any case, these were important questions about *to whom and when to model the learning*, particularly in places where not everyone had experience with rounds. While Sofia and her colleagues were constantly weighing these concerns, people were still sometimes upset by how the task was managed or how the resulting work was shared with others.

## MODELING A LEARNING PROCESS FOR STUDENTS

Addressing the problem of symmetry also means modeling a learning process for students. On one of my first visits in Lakeside, I watched a group of students react with surprise when they entered a library full of animated adults, working in groups with chart paper and sticky notes. When I asked the students if they needed anything, a tenth-grade girl said to me, "I've never seen the library full of teachers at lunch. I usually come in here to talk with my friends. What are they doing?" Instructional rounds may send important messages to students about the learning that is happening between adults in the school. While I did not talk directly with students about rounds, anecdotally, I found them involved with the process in a number of ways. In some of the high schools, students acted as our guides as we went from classroom to classroom for observations. While these students did not enter the classrooms with us for the observations, they were available to answer general questions about the school as we traveled the hallways in between classroom visits. In another high school, a group of students was made available to the entire network to take questions about the school after we discussed the problem of practice and prior to our classroom observations. In this case, the educators were told they could learn something about the school from the students, and the students' message carried weight and authority with our group.

## THE PROBLEM OF SYMMETRY: SOME LESSONS

This chapter has shown that instructional rounds is a cognitively demanding group process that is often ambiguous and sometimes emotionally challenging. Although many Lakeside educators want their students to complete rigorous, challenging tasks that meet these criteria, the educators who practice instructional rounds sometimes have difficulty working with one another on the same kinds of tasks. This suggests strong similarities between instructional rounds and the high-level student tasks that many schools wish their students would complete. In other words, educators can benefit by paying attention to what happens when adults are asked to do this kind of work because it might shed light on how students experience these same types of tasks.

If a district practices instructional rounds regularly and tries to connect that to something like rigor—or raising the level of the task for students—it triggers an equal demand on educators. It demands that they know how to both design and support students in that kind of learning, and rounds is a way to help educators understand that kind of schoolwork. However, if the system does not practice instructional rounds regularly, it probably does not have to deal with this problem, because educators who are uncomfortable can opt out of the experience. School systems that are learning something about high-level tasks through instructional rounds are probably practicing rounds quite frequently and are subsequently dealing with this problem.

By now, it should be obvious that educators do not learn much just by hearing about instructional rounds—they actually have to be regular participants in the task for the data to make sense. Rounds raises important questions about how a system models the learning happening in the network—should everyone in the host school see the patterns and suggestions based on the observation data? Should educators who do not practice see this data? If so, how should the system support their learning from that data? If not, how will the system disseminate what it is learning from instructional rounds? These are questions with which Sofia and her colleagues struggle daily and for which we still don't have answers.

Finally, doing rounds in Lakeside has resulted in at least two ways to think about the relationship between adult and student learning. First, rounds allows educators to participate in a sometimes ambiguous, high-level task that is similar to work that they are hoping students will experience in rigorous classrooms. Second, students and adults have very similar emotional responses to these kinds of high-level tasks. This suggests that instructional rounds is a good guide for thinking about how we can move toward more symmetrical arrangements of adults and students in schools. And we have a new motto for a symmetrical school system: "Don't ask students to do something you're not willing to try yourself!"

## CHAPTER 7

# Helping One Another Learn
## The Problem of Reciprocity

*Tsze-kung asked, saying, "Is there one word
which may serve as a rule of practice for all one's life?"
The Master said, "Is not reciprocity such a word?"*

*—Confucius*

Practicing instructional rounds regularly activates a number of problems to which any leader must attend. The Lakeside Public Schools rounds network now has some ideas about how to address two of those problems: first, how to treat instructional rounds as a regular practice rather than an event (frequency) and, second, how to model learning for each other and for students and to connect the practice of rounds to the best ideas about rigorous instruction (symmetry). With Lakeside developing new ideas about how adults learn, many people in the organization now believe instructional rounds should be the major focus of their improvement work. But what keeps these same people up at night is the subject of this chapter: How will they continue to help one another learn within this system of learning they've created? And how will they know if people are doing anything with that learning? They have reason to be worried—not because they're doing anything wrong, but because many schools and educators have a developed a particular aversion to such commitments, since commitments like these are closely related in their minds to the accountability system that measures students and schools in Lakeside.

Educators' ideas about their professional relationships and commitments to one another in Lakeside have been largely overwhelmed by their experience with the state's performance accountability system. The idea of accountability, whatever the form or meaning that is intended, has become so intertwined with student testing in most educators' minds as to be completely useless for our purposes of adult learning here. In other words, in Lakeside the term *accountability* almost always refers to the tests given to students in most grades and subjects each year—tests that result in each school being given a label based on its students' performance. The value of these accountability ideas in Lakeside or in the U.S. educational system more generally is still an open question, although the ideas probably contribute to the problem we're going to examine in this chapter.[1] Nor does this form of accountability help explain how rounds puts new pressures on the professional relationships of educators within the network and how they learn from one another.

Instead, we'll examine a particular view of educators' professional commitments to one another that has previously been referred to as *lateral accountability*.[2] This idea describes the professional responsibilities and commitments that educators might feel to their colleagues: for example, the professional obligations teachers in a science department might feel toward one another for making sure they each contribute to the planning and execution of the school's new science fair; the responsibility a high school principal has to provide professional development to teachers who are being asked to do more in the classroom, and in turn, those teachers' responsibility for delivering results; or for our purposes here, the professional commitments a network of educators who practice rounds might have to one another.

However, rather than refer to these professional, collegial commitments as lateral accountability, we define it simply as *reciprocity*—literally, a mutual exchange, or in-kind response. One reason to favor the idea of reciprocity over accountability is that an in-kind response is a good way to support learning in an increasingly symmetrical organization—one where the requirements of learning are the same for everyone. Another reason is that it allows us to avoid using the word *accountability* in the Lakeside system, since that word is almost always used in relation to test scores or a system of rewards and punishments delivered at the school level (and, increasingly, toward individual teachers).

Regardless of what one calls it, a system of reciprocal, professional relationships is an extremely difficult thing for schools to put into practice. Reciprocity, as innocuous as it might sound, violates numerous norms and deep traditions of schools. The most enduring of these traditions is that each Lakeside high school has long operated in relative isolation from the other thirty-seven high schools. Instructional rounds immediately puts pressure on this tradition by opening up classrooms and schools to observation and assistance by colleagues from across the district.

In this chapter, we'll look at the problem of reciprocity and try to understand what happened when the network's new expectations conflicted with old ones. At the end, we'll examine a new set of norms and expectations that emerged in Lakeside, in support of reciprocal relationships among the members.

## VISITING OTHER PEOPLE'S SCHOOLS

One important feature of Lakeside's network is that each high school principal and many teacher-leaders are required to visit several other high schools during the academic year. In other words, the boundaries of that network are defined by the high school principals, district staff, and teacher-leaders who share that rounds practice and who have a mandate to visit and work with one another. One can imagine any number of network configurations in a large system like this, and the various configurations might have required various working relationships among educators. For example, the network might have consisted of just district-level administrators. But Lakeside decided to treat all of the high school principals and some of its teacher-leaders as one network, and this design had important implications for how people think about their professional relationships with one another.

The expectations of this network design immediately put pressure on the principals' previous understanding of their relationship with their colleagues, as one principal explained: "We were always kind of in competition with one another before: for students, for resources, and for showing better student performance than the other schools. Rounds are asking something different." In particular, the practice that Sofia and Karen were advocating asked people to support the learning of other people in other schools, and this was sometimes in conflict with the messages people used to get about their work.

Because of the deep traditions of privacy, autonomy, and competition that exist in most high schools, some of the educators involved with instructional rounds had trouble understanding why they needed to leave their own school for rounds and what the benefit might be to them or the system. Mary, a high-school principal, told me about her experiences with the rounds work: "We had a great rounds visit at my school. The data was pretty useful for us. But I don't really see the point of having to go on rounds now at other schools."

What is remarkable about this comment is that many educators from other schools visited Mary's school. In the same breath, Mary appreciates their work, but doesn't necessarily understand why her school might need to reciprocate that effort. Mary's comment does *not* represent a selfish character trait; rather, it represents the repeated influence of a strong culture of isolation and competition that rounds is now pushing against.

One obvious symptom of this culture was that occasionally, principals, district staff, and teacher-leaders decided not to attend their scheduled network visits at the host high school. Given many educators' feeling of competition, this is not surprising. But it did mean that Lakeside had to decide whether or how it was going to deal with attendance problems. Lots of educators noticed that others didn't attend their scheduled rounds days, and this made other people in the network less likely to attend, too, initially creating a negative feedback loop. Importantly, had the system not been practicing rounds on a weekly basis, it probably would not have had to deal with this problem. As I have argued elsewhere, the frequency of the practice of rounds seems to both activate this problem and force people to deal with it at the same time—if the school district hadn't been practicing rounds on a regular basis, Lakeside probably could have ignored the issue.

This attendance issue came to a head during one of the principals' professional development sessions in the first spring of the network's existence. Sofia and some of the other district staff facilitated a discussion about the norms and expectations for the network that day. During the conversation, the principals helped to clarify some of the challenges of the rounds practice, and this helped them all understand why attendance had been poor. Some of the principals explained that they felt that three school visits during the year were too much and that they were spending too much time out of their buildings. They hoped to be able to turn their attention inward, now that they had spent time in other schools. At the same time, other principals said that the "sacrifice" of being out of the building was worth it. This group of principals felt that seeing other people work in other schools was the most beneficial part of the process.

In the end, the network decided that it would keep the expectation for three network visits a year for all principals, and the district compromised by releasing the principals from one of their other monthly professional development sessions. The conversation, regardless of the result, was probably the most important part of the day, as it clarified for everyone both the benefits and the struggles of learning through instructional rounds. Importantly, it brought into sharper relief the expectations that the network would have for one another going forward. Sofia described to me her takeaway from the meeting some time later: "One principal described how [principals] have been pitted against each other in a spirit of competition. We need to change that." Changing that, she imagined, would make them all more willing to spend time helping one another learn.

## WHAT DO WE DO WITH THE OBSERVATION DATA?

These questions of reciprocity also play out in each host school as people become more fluent with the protocols. Even under the best circumstances, each host school was left with a number of challenges about what to do with the data, chart paper, and suggestions after the visitors left. In particular, educators had questions about what the expectations were to implement the recommendations given to the host school during the next level of work. Many network members wondered what both the school and the network were supposed to do after the visit.

Lakeside principals have different ideas about how this follow-up to a rounds day should happen. I spoke with Cynthia, a high school principal with three years of experience. She explained her view of this problem to me in the spring, after almost a full year of rounds in Lakeside:

**Q:** What's your experience of visiting other schools as part of rounds?

**Cynthia:** Well, each time I do it for the district, I feel like the process gets better, there's less waste of time, or it's more clear where we're going. In my experience, it's been nice to see . . . I think it's been helpful for the other schools to get this outside perspective. And I think I'm at a point where I've done enough rounds that maybe it's not necessarily helping in my school at this point, but it will come back to me.

**Q:** What do you mean, it will come back to you?

**Cynthia:** That I'm doing this for other schools, but they will come do this for me as well.

For some of the principals in Lakeside, there is a feeling of diminishing returns the more time they spend practicing instructional rounds in other schools. As participants like Cynthia become familiar with the protocols, some of the freshness begins to wear off, and the real hard part of figuring out what to do next begins.

This makes some principals turn inward to think more carefully about what to do in their own schools. At the same time, Cynthia has internalized the idea that if she wants educators from around the district to do rounds for her, she has to do the same for others.

> Q: I see. You said something very funny, and everybody laughed at the last rounds meeting we were both at. We were talking about the next level of work, and one of the assistant principals [of the host school] was trying to figure out what to do with the data. I think it was one of the first times he had been on rounds, maybe the second time, and he asked some really good questions, and you gave some really good responses about what you might do. And then, at the end you said, "But that's your problem." And everybody laughed.
>
> Cynthia: 'Cause it's true! [laughs].
>
> Q: Yeah, tell me, (a) why you said that, and (b) why do you think people are laughing at that?
>
> Cynthia: [laughs] What I meant was . . . rounds provides data and some suggestions. But the school ultimately is the one that decides what to do with those suggestions. And if it's going to mean anything, the faculty at that school needs to decide what they're going to do with it or if they're going to take those suggestions—and whether they're going to decide as a group to work on this. I mean, I think there's more buy-in when more teachers are seeing the data and making the decisions accordingly than with just one person making the decisions for the staff. But at the end of the day, I can make all the recommendations I want, but it's not something I'm going to take home and lose sleep over. It's something they need to work on as a school. And that's how I interpret what people do around here. People are just coming here to practice doing rounds and leave us with data and an outside perspective, which I value. But it's up to us to decide what we do with that.

Cynthia has aptly described the idea of reciprocity ("it will come back to me"), and yet she also believes it is the host's responsibility to own the data once the visitors leave. In her view, the support that the network gives to a school ends when the rounds visitors leave. But an interesting tension here raises another question: does the network have some professional responsibility to help host schools figure out what to do with the observation data and recommendations? In the terminology in our definition, the question could be restated like this: should there be a mutual exchange of information or knowledge about how to do this stage of improvement work?

The problem of reciprocity has revealed at least two big areas of concern for Lakeside (see exhibit 7.1, "Breaking Old Habits: Tips for Leaders and Instructional Rounds Facilitators" for suggestions on how to handle the two concerns). The first is around the professional norms or expectations that the network might keep. For example, although Sofia and her colleagues had set network norms (at least in name) that included expectations around attendance, people broke these norms anyway. This suggests that the creation of norms and expectations is much less about what the network *says* the norms are and much more about what the network decides to *do* when someone disregards the norms or expectations. In other words, your network can generate as many norms as you want, but people won't believe in them until they see what happens when someone tests them. What you decide to do at that point will say much more about the norms than anything else you do.

The second area of concern has to do with what happens *after* a rounds visit. Elizabeth City and her colleagues don't address this issue directly in their rounds book, but Lakeside has offered at least a couple ways for other school systems to experiment with in their own rounds practice. As described in chapter 2, Sofia gives each principal four options immediately following a day of rounds (figure 2.7 outlined the four options).

The principal of the host school was required to e-mail Sofia and the assistant superintendent his or her chosen option no later than three weeks after a rounds visit. Sofia is not completely satisfied with this approach, but thinks this system of choice and documentation allows schools to experiment with different improvement models while keeping the district office informed about the work. But the district office's responsibility to the host school is not completely clear under this model; there isn't enough time in the day for the district office people to work with every host school after the rounds visit. One could only imagine if each host were supported primarily by the *network*, rather than the district office. The option of coordinating with another school to cross-pollinate the next level of work (detailed in exhibit 7.1 "Breaking Old Habits") seems most likely to encourage that kind of reciprocal relationship. Still, the process of shifting people's thinking and behavior toward that improvement model is a slow one—one that Sofia and her colleagues think about each week after rounds. Another concern is that using documents and forms might make instructional rounds feel like a compliance activity, rather than a learning process. In other words, asking people to fill out a form might make people *less* responsible to the network and more responsible to the central office. Sofia tries to be vigilant in protecting the learning stance of rounds, but she struggles how to gauge that learning in each school when she has so many schools to support.

Finally, this follow-up work will probably become clearer once Lakeside has completed some of the work outlined in part 1: revising its theory of action; articulating the relationship between rounds and rigor; and developing models that describe the relationship between rounds and other improvement processes. That work will serve as a guide for everyone about what the role of rounds is in improvement, and what the schools are supposed to do with the rounds data and suggestions after a school visit. In other words, the follow-up to a network visit should largely be based on a system's theory for how rounds leads to improvement. And that theory of action doesn't become clear unless you try rounds and some of the follow-up work.

I was fortunate to get to see the messy stages of this work and learn a great deal from Lakeside's experiments with instructional rounds. But until this relationship between rounds and other approaches gets clearer, the host schools—and subsequently the network as a whole—will probably continue to have questions about what to do after a day of rounds.

---

### EXHIBIT 7.1

### Breaking Old Habits: Tips for Leaders and Instructional Rounds Facilitators

*Rounds will raise questions about the network members' professional responsibilities to one another. These questions tend to push against strong traditions and old habits that typically exist in large school systems. Leaders and facilitators of rounds can anticipate some of these difficulties and use them as a learning experience for the entire network.*

*Set norms*: Develop norms around attendance and other behaviors that are important for learning, early in the process. Don't be surprised if the network needs to revise and revisit these norms on a regular basis. In short, decide what kinds of issues the network is willing to be flexible on and which issues are non-negotiable. In Lakeside, attendance at three rounds visits was nonnegotiable, and the system was willing to give up other principal meetings in exchange for their attendance at rounds. The network had to make norms and expectations an agenda item at a meeting of all the principals to finally get some traction on this issue. City et al.'s *Instructional Rounds in Education* (Harvard Education Press, 2009) is a good resource on this issue.

*Follow-up*: What happens after a rounds visit can be the most challenging part of the rounds practice. It raises the most difficult questions about the kind of interaction the network should have with the host school after a rounds visit. Lakeside decided to offer the host school four general options and required the school to inform the central office which option it would choose. One of the options draws directly on the idea of reciprocity described in this chapter: Develop a plan with another school to cross-pollinate your next level of work through either of the following:

- Select a school that has a similar problem-of-practice focus question, and collaborate.
- Offer support to a school that has a problem-of-practice focus question in which you have demonstrated strength.

*Make commitments*: Another way to help the network members support one another is to make explicit commitments to each other at the end of a day of instructional rounds. Discuss how the network will support the host and what commitments the host might reasonably keep around the next level of work. Each member of the network should write these commitments on a five-by-seven-inch notecard and place it in his or her own office or in a visible place where the person will see the commitment regularly. Facilitators of rounds can ask the following questions at the end of a day of rounds, to help surface these commitments:

- What one or two commitments can members of the network make that will help the host school learn more about its problem of practice?
- What one or two commitments can the host school make to the network about how the school will continue the work of today?

## THE PROBLEM OF RECIPROCITY: SOME LESSONS

The Lakeside network of educators had to develop, revisit, and revise norms and expectations for instructional rounds—both early in the process and again when it became increasingly clear that they did not all have the same idea about their commitment to rounds. But the network continues to question where its commitments to individual schools begin and end. For example, what should happen after the network visits a school? What responsibility does the school or principal have for reporting back to the network what happened with the data and recommendations? And the network members still have questions about what they should do if a school or an individual does not follow through on what they collectively expect of one another.

In other words, Lakeside has ongoing questions about what level of pressure and support is ideal for the learning expected from rounds. The two follow-up documents that Sofia uses to support that learning serve two distinct purposes: (1) to capture the patterns and recommendations for the host school and (2) to ask the school to articulate its next steps from a menu of choices. As suggested in part 1, this process of recording the data and its subsequent usefulness can have some benefits and drawbacks, particularly if the documentation makes rounds feel like a compliance activity.

The cultural realities of a school system make doing the follow-up work to rounds even harder than it might otherwise be. It's hard enough to figure out what to do with the observation data if the school system is still articulating a theory of action and purpose for rounds. But these difficulties are amplified by the cultural feelings of autonomy and competition that make educators (in this case, the principals in the network) much less likely to know how to assist one another, or why they should, after they are done observing for the day.

To read about all these problems must be discouraging to some readers or at least make some less willing to take on the learning that Sofia and her colleagues struggle with each day. However, if other school systems understand the problems, they may be much more likely to find new, ingenious ways to solve these problems on the path to school improvement. Even these very complex cultural problems of school reform have solutions, and Sofia and her colleagues are on the path to doing just that.

Finally, we've also learned that managing the transition from a state of triage to one of learning really means focusing on both the technical *and* the cultural problems of the system.[3] We've learned that technical solutions about lack of time (the problem of frequency) are fairly straightforward once we allow ourselves to adapt some of the rounds protocols for the time and space that are available to the network. As long as the network protects the nonjudgmental practice of observation and description—always in teams—other parts of the instructional rounds process could no doubt be adapted to meet the needs of a particular school or system schedule. Of course, it's important to actually do all the parts of the process in proper order (description, analysis, prediction, next level of work), but those stages could be compressed or extended, depending on the time available and the experience level of the people doing the practice.

On the other hand, the problems of symmetry and reciprocity are more cultural. They require school systems to pay more careful attention to the relationship between student learning and adult learning (symmetry), and the professional relationships of the rounds network (reciprocity). The Lakeside case demonstrates that managing the transition to adult learning requires that educators name these issues for one another and work through the differences and disagreements that inevitably arise around them.

# PART 3

# Future Challenges

At the beginning of this book, I suggested that Lakeside Public Schools' objectives would be important to consider as we watched the network practice instructional rounds. The most important of those goals, as far as the system is concerned, is closing the achievement gap that is large and persists in the system. This goal is key because Lakeside is measured largely on its ability to narrow the disparate educational outcomes between white students and students of color, and because the superintendent has stated in a widely distributed agenda that closing the gap is a goal. But now that we've looked in detail at the instructional rounds process and the problems that Lakeside is trying to manage, we're left with a significant but perplexing paradox about this goal: one of the reasons Lakeside engages in instructional rounds is to close a racial achievement gap, but educators often have difficulty talking about racial differences in the system during instructional rounds.

This raises a difficult question for any system practicing rounds and interested in affecting student outcomes that differ along racial lines: How do educators understand and deal with racial achievement gaps or other racialized patterns during instructional rounds? What we're learning from Lakeside is that this conversation doesn't happen very often and that, when it does, educators don't always know how to talk to one another. In this chapter, we'll refer to this as the problem of (not) talking about race. Lakeside also isn't unusual in this sense, but how these issues play out here—and how educators, with the best of intentions, attempt these conversations—will be helpful for any school system. And because race remains a controversial and contested topic, we'll make three specific observations that will provide concrete examples of how race and racial differences might be addressed in any school system using rounds. First, conversations about race and student achievement tend to end as quickly as they begin. Second, when the conversations persist, they often result in arguments. And finally, most of the time, these conversations just don't happen, even when educators are confronted with observation data that suggests important racial patterns in the system.

## CHAPTER 8

# The Problem of (Not) Talking About Race

Not everything that is faced can be changed,
but nothing can be changed until it is faced.

—*James Baldwin*

To this point, we've largely ignored how groups of educators talk about race or "achievement gaps" during instructional rounds. Part of the reason for this is that the theory of instructional rounds says that focusing on the *instructional core* (the interaction of students and teachers in the presence of content) gives educators a high-leverage way to describe academic tasks, classroom instruction, and learning. This focus has been incredibly productive for Lakeside Public Schools and is a helpful guide for us. Therefore, one interpretation of this focus could be that the rounds protocols and the instructional core do not ask or require a person to notice the race of the learner or teacher or racial patterns across a system. In that sense, we would stop short of talking about anything other than the task. Under this view, discussing race during rounds could be considered off topic. But this view rests on the assumption that the task and any learning is disconnected from the racial identity of students, for example—or separate from the racial patterns for how students might be identified or grouped across a school system.[1]

However, we know that achievement gaps are important to Lakeside and that this measure of testing is typically disaggregated by race when it is shared with teachers, students, and the broader community. Therefore, another view of rounds and the instructional core is that students and teachers interact in a setting where students are constantly being categorized and placed into groups defined by educators' understanding of race. Those groupings result in patterns that educators sometimes notice during rounds. These patterns can exist in any school system or setting, and while educators sometimes notice them during rounds, they don't always know how to talk about them or suggest how to change these patterns.

Rather than view race as an objective category used to describe groups of people (in this case, Lakeside students), we'll view race and racial achievement gaps as something that educators might observe, discuss, argue about, or even ignore as they discuss what they see in classrooms. Under this view, Lakeside's goal to close achievement gaps using instructional rounds activates important questions that we'll explore here: How does rounds support or limit the ways that educators deal with achievement gaps in the student body? What happens when educators disagree about—or aren't able to discuss—race and racial patterns during rounds? And what might these conversations reveal about how a system might better manage these topics during instructional rounds? As Sofia and her colleagues manage a transition to adult learning in the system, looking at three different ways educators deal with race in Lakeside will also help us think about how other systems might address this issue.

Lakeside begins every instructional rounds visit by examining student performance data disaggregated by race, which often appears in the host school's problem of practice. Lakeside does this because it is focused on figuring out how to solve the problem of disparate outcomes between white students and black and Latino students. In doing rounds, Sofia and her colleagues deal with a very real, very practical dilemma each day: whether or how to support discussions about race and racial differences in the student body. This dilemma probably extends specifically to the high school principals involved in the instructional rounds network. In a survey these principals took at the end of the academic year, more than half of them *disagreed* with the statement "We have *effective* conversations about race and racial inequalities during our professional development sessions." In addition, the principals collectively responded in nearly identical fashion when asked specifically about the instructional rounds process. While they overwhelmingly reported that they understand and support the purpose of the rounds process, more than half of the responding principals *disagreed* with the statement "We talk about race or racial inequalities during the instructional rounds process." On one hand, the principals are charged with disrupting an achievement gap that exists in most schools and in the system. On the other hand, these leaders are not having regular conversations about racial inequalities during their professional development or during instructional rounds. This inconsistency is remarkable, but as we will see shortly, groups of educators sometimes have difficulty having specific conversations about race during the rounds process, and when they do, disagreement often ensues. The disagreement surfaces important, but different assumptions about young people, their capabilities, and educators' responsibility for their learning.

## COMMON CHALLENGES TO TALKING ABOUT RACE

To be clear, Lakeside isn't unusual: many organizations, including all types of schools, have difficulty supporting and managing specific conversations about race and differences in student outcomes. But the patterns to these conversations in Lakeside will be helpful to look at and probably exist in every school system where students and teachers of different racial backgrounds learn and work together. Let's now consider three different conversations.

### 1. Conversations about the racial "achievement gap" tend to end as quickly as they begin.

The most common pattern of conversation when topics of race and the achievement gap come up during instructional rounds is that the conversation can't get off the ground. In the example that follows, Steve, a black administrator in the district, is visiting another high school in the network for instructional rounds. The conference room is filled with fifteen other people who will conduct rounds together on this particular day, and at the moment the network is reading the host school's problem of practice and looking at its achievement data. The data shows large differences in the percentage of students scoring proficient on the tenth-grade state exams between black students and white or Asian students. Steve asks the following question of the whole room: "What do you make of the achievement gap between black students and others?"

It is noticeably quiet for several seconds. Then Eric, a white teacher from the host school, offers this response to Steve's question: "We don't really think about instruction for black students versus instruction for Asian or white students."

Steve says, "I think other schools will want to know . . . Schools will want to know what your theory is for why scores of some students improved while others did not."

After Steve's response to Eric, the conversation takes a turn to a different topic, and that is the end of their exchange. This example is telling for at least two reasons.

First, because the conversation is happening in front of a large group of educators who are trying to figure out what they are supposed to pay attention to when they observe in classrooms, it will affect what educators will later observe and discuss today. The network is discussing the host school's problem of practice, which signals to the observers where the school thinks it is struggling and what it wants the observers to focus on when they take notes. In this particular example, Eric and Steve's exchange has put black, white, and Asian students on the table, but without any resolution about whether this topic is relevant for the upcoming observations. Second, Eric thinks that teachers in the school don't think about the race of their students, but Steve does. This in itself probably warrants discussion before educators step into classrooms today. But Steve also wants to talk about the patterns in achievement in this school—why instruction is apparently more effective for some students than others. Their exchange ends without any resolution to this tension.

**2. When these conversations do persist, they often result in disagreement that surfaces important assumptions about students.**

Jamie and Taylor are colleagues in the same math department in the same high school. This high school also shows a discrepancy in educational outcomes between white students and students identified as black or Latino. Jamie, who is white, teaches an algebra II course for students who will likely go on to pre-calculus, and many of those students will attend college. Most of the students in her class are white or Asian. Taylor, who is also white, teaches a course for sophomore students: algebra B. Most of these students will take only one more math class in high school, and none of them will take pre-calculus. Most of the students in Taylor's classes are black or Latino.

Jamie and Taylor have just finished analyzing the rounds data from their own school, where both were participants on different rounds teams today. Near the end of the discussion on the next level of work, Jamie says, "We have students who have the ability to think at a high level. We have students who are more comfortable at lower levels. At some point in their lives, something got lost and now there's a huge gap."

It's difficult to know what Jamie is trying to explain here. It's possible that when she says that "something got lost," she's saying that students' lives outside of school make learning difficult for them. Or she may think that students who are "more comfortable at lower levels" require a particular kind of math content. Whatever her intended meaning, her statement doesn't sit well with Taylor. She responds quickly from the other side of the table: "I think we should distinguish between their ability for higher-order, complex thinking and their academic achievement."

Right away there is tension in the air, because this is the first signal of real disagreement in the room today. To this point, there has been almost no disagreement about the rounds data or the patterns that the rounds teams have identified today. But there's something different about this exchange, because these colleagues are now generating theories about why there are different outcomes among students. The rounds teams have agreed that most of the tasks they observed today were in the lower third of Bloom's taxonomy (remember, understand, apply)—even in some AP classes. Despite this consistency across the school, some students are clearly doing better than others. But that data doesn't enter this conversation at this point, either. Jamie tries to continue the conversation by generating a theory: "The kids would be able to handle higher-order thinking if—"

Taylor cuts her off: "You teach advanced math and I teach the developing algebra kids, and you're telling me we can't pull material from one class to another?" Taylor is visibly angry now and wants no part of Jamie's theory. Taylor seems to think that her students are capable of doing the work of a higher-level math course, like Jamie's course.

Jamie responds coolly, but firmly, "You teach yours, I'll teach mine."

These teachers have known each other for at least an entire school year, teaching in the same department all that time. But this conversation has surfaced different perspectives on their students' learning, and the two women are unable to talk about this disagreement, even though both have observed many of the same classrooms today. Their experience with their own classrooms may be influencing their understanding of what they see across the school, but we don't know this for sure, because the tension between them has made it hard to understand clearly what is happening. This disagreement isn't necessarily a bad result, if they trust each other enough to have the conversation again. But because they also won't practice rounds again for some time, that follow-up may have to happen in another type of meeting or setting. Whatever the case, this disagreement is instructive because it shows that people who might share a common school and department experience can still have very different views and explanations of the disparate student outcomes in their school. Alternatively, perhaps their views are more similar than they know, but the sensitivity and anxiety of talking about students and their abilities gets in the way. Either way, it's clear that Jamie and Taylor have more to talk about if they are going to continue to work together in their department this year.

**3.  Most of the time, these conversations just don't happen—even when educators notice or question structural factors that might result in important racial patterns.** Occasionally, educators make connections between race and student course-taking patterns. This kind of observation data is important because it can be direct evidence for systemic or school-based patterns that affect achievement outcomes. In these cases, an educator might describe the composition of a classroom in terms of the race of the students. In the following example, this group of educators have just finished reading their sticky notes that recorded their classroom observations, during the debrief portion of the rounds protocol. They have all observed the same four classrooms today and are now thinking about how they will organize the sticky notes and what patterns might exist. Carla, who is white, begins this portion of the conversation: "I noticed that most of the kids in the AP class were white girls."

No one in the group says anything for a full five seconds. Finally Vanessa, who is also white, asks, "What did you think of the lesson?"

Carla replies, "I'm not sure. I was just noticing that. What did you think?"

"I noticed that they were working on the Revolutionary War," Vanessa says.

Robert says, "Right, the siege of Charleston."

Although the school is quite racially diverse, Carla has noticed that most of the students in one AP course are white. Rather than engage Carla's comment and either share a similar observation about the racial makeup of the class or contradict Carla with different evidence about the classroom or school, Vanessa starts a completely new line of inquiry. Perhaps Vanessa doesn't have any evidence to add to Carla's comment, or perhaps she has ignored it. But this is a typical result when educators share racialized patterns like Carla's, and so the conversation never really happens. The group's chart paper gets organized without any mention of Carla's observation.

## MANAGING CONVERSATIONS ABOUT RACE AND ACHIEVEMENT

Although Lakeside doesn't have a systemic solution for supporting these types of conversations yet, some Lakeside educators are starting to think about this problem. A racially diverse team of teachers in one school has identified a process for trying to unearth some of the different perspectives on race and achievement among educators, prior to beginning the instructional rounds process. They are doing this in part because they feel that instructional rounds assumes a "threshold belief" in students and their abilities that this team of educators does not think currently exists in all the educators in Lakeside. In particular, they believe that all educators' assumptions about race, poverty, and family background play a role in the educators' beliefs about students' ability to learn. In response, the team has developed a process for doing shared reading and discussion about students, their families, and educators' responsibility for student learning. The approach is meant to anticipate and discuss the different beliefs of educators before anyone steps into classrooms for observation during rounds. This group of educators is supporting these topics by assigning shared reading for the educators interested in rounds in their school, prior to beginning a school-based version of the rounds process. They plan to read "Cultivating a School-Based Discourse That Emphasizes Teachers' Responsibility for Student Learning," an article by John Diamond, who is a sociologist of education and studies the relationship between social inequality and educational opportunity.[2] Nathan, one of the educators on this team, explains Diamond's article in this way: "[The article] is very disarming and rich and includes a lot of very strong evidence about how when teachers in urban schools focus on practice and instruction, and focus teacher talk around that, rather than the perceived deficits of students, that the results are better. I'm not doing [the article] justice. But before we even go into a classroom, we're going to read this article and talk about that because I think there needs to be this threshold belief that you acknowledge that what you do, the work you give, matters . . . So that's where we're starting."

Diamond's article provides a framework for talking about teaching and learning, with the following two goals in mind: (1) to emphasize teachers' responsibility for student learning and (2) to challenge arguments that blame students or their families for a "supposed lack of educational investment." As quoted above, Nathan thinks the article will help the group members "focus on practice and instruction." At first glance, this suggests that they won't necessarily focus on race directly. However, this focus will likely help them unearth and manage educators' assumptions about students' families more directly. Such an approach constitutes an important part of managing a conversation in the context of Lakeside's goals for closing achievement gaps.

In the article, Diamond proposes that groups of educators try to respond and role-play around the following question: "How might you reframe a conversation about low test scores, after a colleague made a statement blaming students and their families for these scores?"

Diamond suggests that the purpose of the role-play is to practice responding to one's colleagues, without blaming or making people feel isolated. Given how these kinds of conversations can end in argument, this might be a helpful stance for Lakeside to take. Another potentially helpful part of this process is that it helps educators reframe conversations to keep the focus on the responsibility of educators to provide rigorous instruction. Finally, this kind of approach might be effective if it helps provide educators with common language for talking about students and their achievement. In this way, this exercise anticipates the kinds of conversations that tend to result in arguments in Lakeside, and engages educators in a practice that is analogous to rounds.

## A PROTOCOL: EMPHASIZING EDUCATORS' RESPONSIBILITY FOR STUDENT LEARNING

At the moment, Lakeside has not widely adopted a process or protocol for supporting these conversations. However, since Lakeside already has a tradition of using the first half hour of a day of instructional rounds to discuss the system's theory of action, at some point the network could use that time to do something similar to what the teacher team has suggested above. Exhibit 8.1, "A Twenty-Five-Minute Protocol for Emphasizing Educators' Responsibility for Student Learning," is meant to generate conversations about educators' responsibility for student learning, using Diamond's article and the teacher teams' suggestions.

The point here is that if rounds is to provide an opening to talk about racial differences or racialized classroom patterns in productive ways, then leaders will need to provide educators with a way of starting that conversation. Just as rounds facilitators provide a theory and protocol for focusing on the instructional core, school systems that want to close achievement gaps will need to provide some kind of theory and protocol for framing (or in many cases, reframing) discussions about race, achievement, and educators' responsibility for student learning during instructional rounds.

Importantly, there are many texts and protocols for supporting this kind of work, and we've only examined one here. In recent conversations with other educators about this issue, another book that has been recommended more than once is *Doing Race* (W. W. Norton, 2010). This recent collection of twenty-one essays edited by Hazel Rose Markus and Paula M. L. Moya may have one specific advantage in that it takes the reader outside schools and into a variety of everyday situations. This approach may initially be more appealing to a group of educators if they are able to consider these topics outside their school for a moment. Although the book is targeted to undergraduates, its lessons would be useful for a wide range of educators and system leaders.

---

**EXHIBIT 8.1**

## A Twenty-Five-Minute Protocol for Emphasizing Educators' Responsibility for Student Learning

1. As a group, first read silently "Focusing on Student Learning," by John Diamond (ten minutes). This three-page article is in *Everyday Antiracism: Getting Real About Race in School* (New Press, 2008), edited by Mica Pollack. There are a number of other articles that would work well, but the idea here is to use texts of no more than three pages. In this way, the protocol can be repeatedly used with the rounds network before school visits without taking too much time away from classroom observations.

2. Next, using the following discussion questions from the article as a prompt, turn and talk to a partner (five minutes).
   - "To what extent do you agree that it is important for educators to accept more responsibility for student learning and achievement?"
   - "How can educators do this without feeling blamed?"

   Another reason for using this protocol and these prompts before rounds is that it signals to the network that these questions are relevant during rounds, and it provides the group with common language for that discussion.

3. Then, as a whole group, discuss the article's strategy question (five minutes): "Consider a type of challenge some of your students face. How might you and your colleagues better start to address that challenge?" The focus of instructional rounds is the *system*, not individual schools or teachers, and this question helps to put that focus back on the network, rather than on "problem" educators or schools.

4. Finally, turn back to your partner to role-play Diamond's "things to try tomorrow" (five minutes): "How might you reframe a conversation about low test scores, after a colleague made a statement blaming students and their families for those scores?" Role-play that interaction.

## THE PROBLEM OF (NOT) TALKING ABOUT RACE: SOME LESSONS

Racially diverse groups of educators will probably not be able to talk about or deal with race or related ideas of the achievement gap directly during instructional rounds without support. This is a problem of adult learning in any system that is interested in closing racial achievement gaps or using instructional rounds to help it do so. Like the other problems in this book, the reluctance to discuss race isn't created by instructional rounds, but rounds does bring the problem into sharper focus as educators discuss evidence gathered across the system. Just as educators sometimes need educational frameworks to help them give language and meaning to classroom tasks (think Bloom's Taxonomy), educators will likely need language and frameworks to help them make sense of racialized classroom patterns ("most of the kids in the AP class were white girls") or about race more generally ("the black-white achievement gap").

One danger to make explicit here is that without better support and processes for "doing race," some educators of color may feel a significant burden to carry these discussions.[3] In fact, it should be the entire instructional rounds network's responsibility for discussing these patterns, if the network so chooses, rather than the role of any one person or group of people. But other educators may struggle because they may want to discuss race and the achievement gap, but do not know how, or feel uncomfortable doing so. Understanding these different perspectives—and the typical patterns for how these conversations often happen—makes it more likely that any school system might better manage the learning that people are trying to do across the rounds network. Providing specific support makes it more likely that educators will feel successful when they do so.

In most school systems, diversity programs meant to help educators think about race and the role it plays in a school or classrooms are one-off events, separate from any instructional improvement programs happening in the system. However, the examples in this chapter suggest that the educators practicing instructional rounds need protocols and specific language for talking about race, achievement, and teachers' responsibility for student learning. Even within the structured, carefully managed protocols of the rounds process, the different perspectives on race, the achievement gap, and educators' responsibility for student learning that naturally exist among educators can overwhelm their collective ability to deal with these topics. Quite simply, one should not expect rounds teams to have productive conversations around these topics unless the system provides them with this support. Any school system will likely need to treat the learning they do about race and racial differences much like they do rounds—as a process that needs to be managed and supported in a variety of ways over time. In fact, any school system that puts a demand on educators for closing achievement gaps probably activates an equal demand on that system to provide educators with language and knowledge for talking about the problem in productive ways. In short, a system that doesn't provide that support may be requiring a collective set of expectations and understanding about student learning that doesn't exist in any system.

## CHAPTER 9

# Learning from Systemic Problems

At the beginning of this book, I suggested that the instructional rounds process would likely disrupt the typical patterns of interaction of Lakeside Public Schools educators and that some of this disruption would be a good thing. Instructional rounds initially gives educators a process and protocol for doing classroom observations in teams—a way that is very different from how they have previously done business. The Lakeside example has shown that this disruption comes with other consequences. In particular, it reveals broader systemic problems, which educators do not have a lot of experience in solving.

Besides revealing these systemic problems, Lakeside has also demonstrated for us how this adult learning process challenges deep traditions of schooling and school reform that we've had to consider along the way. First, rounds violates numerous cultural norms of privacy and autonomy of schools and classrooms. The idea of spending time in one another's classrooms and schools directly challenges these norms. Second, instructional rounds tends to conflict with some of the more common structural arrangements of schooling that make working in teams and large networks quite difficult. Like nearly all school districts in this country, Lakeside's largely bureaucratic, hierarchical arrangement was in conflict with the flat, mostly role-neutral arrangement of the instructional rounds network the district intended. Third, the work of instructional rounds happens on top of layer upon layer of other school reform efforts in places like Lakeside. As a result, teachers and other educators have good reason to be skeptical that instructional rounds might offer them something better than or different from the other reforms they have already endured.

However, by seeing rounds in this context, we've been able to think about how Lakeside might adapt its school system—and in some cases practice rounds differently—to solve these problems. In more practical terms, we've tried to address the question that is at the heart of a school district's dilemma: How does a system manage a transition to adult learning, when that process conflicts with the previous ways we've done business? In other words, how do we move from a state of triage to one of learning? Bearing all of this in mind, let's review some of the lessons of instructional rounds. First, we'll look at some broad lessons that have emerged. Then, we'll review each chapter. Finally, the book will end with some specific recommendations for school systems that are practicing instructional rounds.

## FOCUS ON THE SYSTEM

This book focused primarily on the systemic problems of large-scale adult learning in the service of instructional improvement. I've tried to document the role that rounds might play in revealing, disrupting, or reinforcing those problems. We've also seen how rounds is initially a difficult, uncomfortable thing for many educators and that some of this difficulty can be managed by facilitators and leaders if they carefully structure the environment in which educators work before, during, and after classroom observations. Strong protocols for each stage allow educators to get quite adept at rounds, and several Lakeside schools are getting pretty good at doing just that. In fact, many educators report that they really enjoy rounds as they become more comfortable with the process. But that doesn't mean that they've shifted the culture of the system toward adult learning, simply because people are doing rounds. Here's why they need to remain vigilant: if the Lakeside high schools do instructional rounds in relative isolation from one another, they risk having thirty-eight different improvement strategies simultaneously enacted across the school system. What this looks like is something akin to thirty-eight people trying to get a large bolder rolling by pushing from thirty-eight different directions—no one is going anywhere. Instead, this book focused on the learning and relationships of the educators in the rounds network, rather than individual school sites, because the network is designed to confront the isolated nature of schools and better approximates the experience of the system as a whole.

## PRACTICE FIRST, THEN PRACTICE SOME MORE—EVALUATE LATER

Besides focusing on the system as a whole, we've also spent a lot of time describing several other problems associated with instructional rounds in Lakeside, rather than evaluating the effort. This may feel discouraging at first for some readers. Many who practice rounds initially want to know if they are doing it "right," and how they will know if it "works." Naturally, many of us as educators are predisposed to look first for solutions that we think might help us get better at our work—we often don't have time for anything more. We have to understand, though, that there is a strong tendency for all of us to implement solutions (and instructional rounds) without a clear or widely shared understanding of the common problems we face. As a different educational example, this country has now gone through at least two waves of the small-school movement, whose proponents claim that smaller schools will outperform larger ones. Many school systems created numerous small schools. Unfortunately, there's absolutely no evidence that on average, small schools outperform larger ones consistently. Further, it's not clear exactly what problem this solution was meant to solve. One common argument was that students would feel more connected to smaller schools, but even if they do, this strategy has yet to repeatedly produce consistent average gains across large school systems. This example is one of just many in our collective education reform history. Given this history, I tried to describe and understand the practice of rounds, rather than evaluate whether Lakeside is doing it right.

## VIEWING PROBLEMS AS OPPORTUNITIES FOR ORGANIZATIONAL LEARNING

In his papers on workplace learning, Paul Hager discusses the limitations of viewing professional development as a set of skills or characteristics, arguing that it treats learning "as a product" based on "previous formal learning experiences."[1] For example, one of the ways educators learn through instructional rounds is by gaining experience with the rounds protocols. However, getting good at the discrete skills of these protocols is only one step in a much longer process that is fraught with difficulties. Rather than focusing on discrete skills, Hager advocates for a view of workplace learning that is "problematic." A problematic view of instructional rounds means that the process should constantly create new questions if people are learning anything. As we saw in chapter 3, one of the ways educators can do this is by developing problems of practice that allow observers to focus on a particular instructional problem. Educators use problems of practice to observe, discuss, and ultimately revise their original statements about their instructional problems. Following in this tradition, we've also looked at a set of broader problems that tend to emerge during rounds. The indicators summarized in exhibit

9.1, "Instructional Rounds: Indicators of Learning," and discussed further in the next sections are adapted from some of Hager's work and serve as an example of the kinds of questions that come up when educators practice instructional rounds. Other school systems might also find them useful as indicators of learning if they decide to use instructional rounds as part of a larger school reform effort.

**1. Instructional rounds will raise questions about the rules or patterns for how educators typically interact with one another.** Finding a way to structure teachers' workdays so that people can learn in teams every week is an important technical challenge that Lakeside needed to solve. One of the first problems Lakeside confronted when it practiced instructional rounds is precisely this technical problem: How do we make time and space for educators to regularly learn together in groups? (This is the problem of *frequency.*) It turns out that the answer to the question is sometimes in conflict with some of the rules and patterns for how educators usually spend time with one another.

**2. Instructional rounds will raise questions about the relationship between adult and student learning.** For example, educators in Lakeside regularly express a desire to see students complete more rigorous school work. By *rigorous*, they typically mean school tasks where students are able to have conversations with one another, use academic language, and produce individual or group products that show command of the academic language and an understanding of how different concepts relate to one another. Educators say such tasks are difficult because they can require multiple steps or routes to arrive at an answer and can be emotionally challenging for students. However, many teachers initially dislike instructional rounds for the very reasons that make it a rigorous task: the rounds work can be ambiguous and emotionally challenging. Educators often work in an environment where they have very little experience doing the kinds of tasks that they wish their students would do. Thus, one of the problems that Lakeside had to confront was both a technical and cultural one: How will the learning we do as adults model the type of learning that we expect of students? (This is the problem of *symmetry.*) While it might be reasonable to expect educators in any role (teacher, principal, superintendent) to participate in the kinds of learning they expect of their students, this is not as easy as it sounds.

**3. Instructional rounds will raise questions about the social, cultural, and political realities of educators' work life.** Many educators have difficulty understanding how or why they might reciprocate the learning that happens during visits to other

## EXHIBIT 9.1

### Instructional Rounds: Indicators of Learning

*The regular practice of instructional rounds tends to raise important questions about a school system. Facilitators, school leaders, and other participants of instructional rounds can anticipate these questions and use them as discussion points for the network's learning.*

1. Instructional rounds will raise questions about the rules or patterns for how educators have typically interacted with one another on the job:
   • How are we supposed to make time for instructional rounds?
   • Will instructional rounds replace something else we're doing?
   • How will we do rounds under our current contract, agreement, or labor situation?

2. Instructional rounds will raise questions about the relationship between adult and student learning:
   • Is instructional rounds a model for something else we could be doing in classrooms?
   • If so, what does that look like?
   • What kind of learning is appropriate or effective for adults, and how does that differ from the learning that students might do?

3. Instructional rounds will raise questions about the social, cultural, and political realities of educators' work life:
   • Why do we need to visit other schools?
   • Why do outsiders need to visit our school?
   • What's our responsibility to a host school, after we leave?

4. Instructional rounds will raise questions about previous judgments or evaluations of schools and educators in the system:
   • Why does this school have higher test scores than that school?
   • Why do we see the same instructional patterns across all of our schools?
   • Who is evaluating our schools or teachers, and have these evaluators observed what we've observed?

*Source:* Adapted from Paul Hager's papers on workplace learning. See, for example, Paul Hager, "Conceptions of Learning and Understanding Learning at Work." *Studies in Continuing Education* 26, no. 1 (March 2004).

schools. The problem of *reciprocity* is largely a cultural problem that contains a particular view of accountability: How will we help one another learn in the system of learning that we have created? And how will we know if anyone is doing anything with that learning? When educators in this school system are asked (and sometimes required) to help each other learn, the organization is doing something that is heavily countercultural. Helping one another learn often conflicts with school-level accountability systems in play at many schools: one in which the educators often believe the schools are being measured against one another. Rounds often prompts educators to start asking questions about these realities, given that the practice runs counter to the competitive culture of some systems and external accountability systems more generally.

**4. Instructional rounds will raise questions about previous judgments or evaluations of schools and educators in the system.** An example for this fourth indicator is that Lakeside educators are starting to notice the same instructional pattern across the thirty-eight high schools, regardless of the school's accountability status or relative standing in the school district. In other words, some of the Lakeside high schools have a reputation for being "good" schools, while others have less sterling reputations. However, the pattern of instruction emerging across all of those schools is remarkably consistent. In short, there is a clear pattern of students being asked to do what Lakeside calls lower-level tasks (e.g., remember, understand, apply) and relatively few higher-level tasks (e.g., synthesize, evaluate, or create), even in schools that are widely considered good schools.

Taken together, these questions show that instructional rounds can place new pressures on the school system, activate problems the system didn't know it had, and force the educators to realize that they don't necessarily know what to do next. Being in this state is probably a good thing, but to the people doing the work, it can sometimes feel as if they are standing together on a ledge, trying to convince one another to take a leap into the unknown.

## TECHNICAL PROBLEMS OF SCHOOL SYSTEMS

In chapters 1 and 2, we saw that educators can develop some common understanding about what they are seeing across classrooms in a school or system, but this takes many hours of in-depth discussion and analysis of the data and a skilled facilitator who understands how to get educators to describe what they saw using specific, nonjudgmental language. Although the educators who participated in

Lakeside's rounds learned something about the school (and each other) while working with one another, they also left the process mentally fatigued. Others were not necessarily pleased or satisfied with the patterns and recommendations the group generated. In short, convincing educators that this process might be worth doing on a regular basis is no easy task.

The detailed example of the rounds process in chapters 1 and 2 illustrates a set of immediate reasons why it is initially difficult and maybe even unpleasant for some educators to practice rounds. The reasons include previously poor experiences with walk-throughs and other classroom observation programs; a lack of common language or knowledge of instructional problems; and especially an infrequent emphasis on the learning of adults in the system and processes like rounds, where that learning is supposed to happen.

In chapter 3, we addressed the question "Why rounds?" In other words, what motivates educators, and the system more broadly, to use the process? In short, we saw that part of adult learning is really about generating and revising improvement theories in ways that people can understand and act upon. More generally, just because educators do classroom observations together as part of the rounds process, they don't all understand or support the process in the same way. There is a great deal of work that has to happen before and after rounds to create a common vision for the system's improvement goals.

In chapter 4, we saw that many schools that start the rounds process have difficulty identifying and describing a problem of practice, initially locating their problems in students or in broader society. This has two important implications for school systems and leaders using instructional rounds. First, because writing a problem of practice is developmental, leaders need to pay attention to where a school is in that process and provide appropriate pressure and support, rather than a one-size-fits-all approach. Second, educators should be involved in the writing and revision of a problem of practice, since the learning that occurs in that process is as important as the observing in classrooms. This is an important idea both for educators practicing instructional rounds and for those interested in school reform more generally. First, as if rounds weren't countercultural enough already, the idea that classroom observations aren't really a complete form of professional development may be difficult for systems to consider. And this finding may fly in the face of the most ardent supporters of instructional rounds. Getting into classrooms to observe violates cultural norms of the autonomy of educators, and observing in cross-role teams is largely unheard-of in the typical, hierarchical arrangements of school systems. The idea, then, that classroom observations—which are so countercultural in the first place—might not be enough to help the typical educator improve will not be popular with some supporters of instructional rounds or with the school reformers who advocate similar classroom observation processes meant to open up the classroom for analysis.

In chapter 5, we looked at the first of the more systemic problems, the problem of frequency. This is a technical challenge mostly having to do with finding the time to train and allow people to practice rounds regularly. In response to this problem, Lakeside educators are adapting the rounds protocol to increase the frequency with which people observe in teams. This is an important change, because it's one of the first examples of how Lakeside is changing rounds, rather than simply adapting to the model of instructional rounds. And this is not surprising—the history of school reform is full of examples of how educators adapt and change the programs and processes of school reformers to meet their own needs or understandings of the reform. That schools within systems might use their own school-based version of rounds is not surprising, given this history. But school systems will need to maintain a focus on systemic improvement and a coherent message about the purpose of rounds so that those school-based efforts do not undermine the systemic effort.

Additionally, school systems should be aware that these school-based adaptations of the rounds protocols will affect how educators learn. While a district rounds process can likely commit just one day to a school site during the year, individual schools may be able to use some adaptation of the process much more frequently. As school sites compress or expand the amount of time educators practice each stage of rounds, those adaptations will vary across schools. Paying attention to these adaptations is important for maintaining a coherent, system-wide learning goal. In addition, professional development in this school system is increasingly connected to the work and learning that people are doing in the rounds network. Educators and professional development providers have regular contact with both the rounds protocols and the observation data as part of that professional development. Professional development, like Lakeside's rigor course, is an incubator for teacher-leaders to become instructional rounds facilitators. However, neither a focus on rigor, a rigor course, nor instructional rounds by itself is an improvement strategy. In other words, one of these processes alone probably will not help a school system shift to a model of adult learning. But a comprehensive model of how rounds, rigor, and professional development fit together might support that kind of change if the system can develop theories for how they are related to one another and support a focus on instructional improvement.

## CULTURAL PROBLEMS OF SCHOOL SYSTEMS

As we moved from the problem of frequency to other systemic problems, we saw that these challenges were increasingly cultural, rather than the more technical problem of time we examined in chapter 5. In chapter 6, we looked at the first of these primarily cultural problems: symmetry. Rounds is a challenging, high-level adult task that can be ambiguous and emotionally challenging. However, school systems are increasingly asking how they can support students in these types of challenging classroom tasks. Rounds is one way to demonstrate some of the similarities between adult and student learning, and making these connections for adults may help the system to better understand and support student learning. In other words, in a symmetric organization, the requirements and types of learning are similar across roles and levels of the organization, and there are strong similarities between the learning of adults and that of students.

In chapter 7, we learned that the members of the rounds network will have questions about how to support one another's learning, and where those commitments to helping one another begin and end. In systems where schools are often in competition with one another, the transition to a reciprocal exchange of ideas and support requires careful attention to developing, revisiting, and revising expectations for educators participating in the rounds process. In addition, school systems will need to develop ways to encourage schools to use the rounds data to inform professional development and to partner with other schools as they do so. Lakeside is experimenting with several documents meant to support this kind of mutual exchange, including one that captures all of the patterns and recommendations for the host school and asks the host to outline the next steps for improvement. On one hand, principals report that they appreciate being able to look back at the patterns and recommendations from rounds over the course of several school visits by examining these documents. On the other hand, there may be some danger that asking the school to record and report the next steps makes rounds look or feel like a compliance activity—something that Sofia has tried hard to avoid. But she suggests that giving schools a variety of options, particularly ones that allow schools and principals to collaborate with one another after a rounds visit, is both technically and culturally very different from the way the district went about school improvement and monitoring in the past.

Finally in chapter 8, we looked at a problem to which the school system has few solutions at the moment. While educators practicing rounds in this system need protocols and specific language for talking about race, achievement, and teachers' responsibility for student learning, the rounds process does not seem to be the structure within which those conversations can happen, at least in its current form. Even within the structured, carefully managed protocols of rounds, the different perspectives that educators naturally bring to the process overwhelm their collective ability to deal with data that are racialized or about achievement gaps in the system. Quite simply, one should not expect rounds teams to have productive conversations around these topics unless the system provides them with support. The school system's demand for closing achievement gaps probably activates an equal demand on the system to provide educators with language and knowledge for actually talking about this problem. In short, the system is requiring a collective set of expectations for student learning that currently does not exist in the system. In the meantime, educators' individual, default beliefs and expectations for student learning will likely trump any collective problem solving of their interest in racial achievement gaps in the system.

Much of this confirms the work of others who have investigated large-scale instructional improvement efforts. Still, there are some practical considerations worth stating here for both the process of rounds and large-scale improvement more generally.

First, it may be more productive for educators using rounds in the early stages to think of the process as one that uncovers problems, rather than one that solves them. This idea may seem counterintuitive, for several reasons. First, the educators in Lakeside have shown that they really do want answers to their problems, which makes it difficult for them to suspend that particular stance while the rounds process is rolled out across the system. Second, rounds itself invites some level of problem solving early in the process, through the next-level-of-work stage, when educators typically offer recommendations of support to the host school. But the Lakeside case has shown that if the system regularly practices rounds in multiple schools over an academic year, the process reveals broader problems that probably need to be solved concurrent with the rounds process—if it is to result in improvement. Importantly, the thirty-eight principals in this school system are probably learning something from each other about these problems because of the frequency of the practice and the increasing regularity of the contact between principals, central office staff, and classroom teachers during the rounds process.

At the same time, the system probably is not learning much about achievement gaps at the moment because educators typically do not have specific language at their disposal for talking about race or racialized classroom patterns. The rounds process seems unlikely to help educators notice or disrupt the structural characteristics of the school system that allow these racialized patterns to continue, even as it helps educators focus on aspects of teaching and learning.

## BUILDING ON THE PRACTICE OF INSTRUCTIONAL ROUNDS

The Lakeside school district has adapted the instructional rounds process in several ways that are worth considering here before we end. First, I'll review these since these changes or extensions to the rounds practice described by City et al. in *Instructional Rounds* are adaptations that other systems will want to consider. Then, I'll offer some suggestions for how a school system might build on instructional rounds to better address racialized classroom data and patterns.

### Create specific protocols for sharing and revising theories of action.

At least two protocols emerged in Lakeside and were meant to help answer the question "Why rounds?" One of these protocols allowed Sofia to share the system's theory of action at the beginning of each day of rounds and get feedback on the theory from classroom teachers and other school-based personnel. However, this statement was probably too abstract for most educators during the early stages of the rounds process, and so Sofia and her colleagues developed additional graphic models showing the relationship between rounds and other improvement processes in the system. In chapter 3, I offered a protocol that might assist Lakeside and other systems with developing the relationships between rounds and these other processes and using those to revise the system-level theory of action.

### Differentiate support for problems of practice.

The Lakeside case shows that if given support and opportunity, educators can revise a problem of practice. As we have learned, schools at different stages will need different kinds of support (chapter 4). Much of this has to do with where schools locate their problems, as they move from the initial stage (problem not specified) to the emerging stage (located in students) to the evolving stage (located in the organization).

**Invite classroom teachers into the regular revision of problems of practice.**
Since problems of practice do seem to be developmental with the right kinds of support, most of the adult learning that needs to happen actually happens in between rounds days, not during classroom observations. The bulk of the professional development of instructional rounds happens when educators discuss the problem of practice in light of the most recent observation data, not during the creation of the sticky notes and charts that are the typical product of instructional rounds. In other words, we shouldn't expect educators to change their classroom practice if they aren't also part of the revision of the problem of practice on a regular basis. Thus, part of the practice of instructional rounds means managing educators' expectations about what they might gain from classroom observations and why the observations might not be the only part of the practice in which they should participate.

**Adapt the protocols for time (frequency)—but protect the nonjudgmental practice.**
School-based rounds is increasingly how principals in the network plan to share the practice within their schools to increase the frequency of rounds. This is an important development as this practice is emerging outside Lakeside's original rounds network, but will likely influence how people understand and practice rounds across the system. Some Lakeside principals developed a process and staffing plan for scheduling teachers into observation groups for a school-based version of rounds. Teachers volunteered their planning periods several times a semester to free up time without requiring substitute teachers. This plan requires that the rounds teams meet after school, and sometimes several days after making the classroom observations. This is a trade-off that the principals have to weigh: adaptation of rounds in this way can create more opportunities for people to practice observing in teams, while losing some of the freshness of the data for the debrief.

The problem of frequency has also shown that doing rounds in the Lakeside has disrupted the typical ways educators work with one another. Rounds has made principals and teachers reallocate time within the daily schedule for the purpose of observation and discussion of instructional practice. The degree of disruption is inextricably linked with the frequency of rounds. The typical rules or patterns that govern educators' time are not always compatible with rounds, but these are the very patterns that educators begin to question once they practice rounds regularly.

### Make clear connections between rounds and high-level student tasks (symmetry).

In many ways, instructional rounds is the kind of high-level task educators wish their students could complete (chapter 6). These kinds of tasks can be ambiguous and emotionally challenging for anyone. System leaders and facilitators can anticipate some of these difficulties and use them as a learning experience for the entire network: With practice, these discussions can form the basis for thinking about how adults can model the types of learning they might want for students.

### Develop specific follow-up expectations and practices that implicate the network in everyone's learning (reciprocity).

Rounds will raise questions about the network members' professional responsibilities to the learning of one another. These questions tend to push against strong traditions and old habits that typically exist in large school systems. Leaders and facilitators of rounds can anticipate some of these difficulties and use them as a learning experience for the entire network.

One consistent question about the rounds practice has to do with the next level of work—what should the host school do with the recommendations and data? The problem of reciprocity demonstrates that educators in a network often don't have a lot of experience helping one another learn, and this makes members of network less likely to follow up with the host school once the school visit is over. This puts a large demand on traditional structures (e.g., the central office) that probably don't have the capacity to help each school. Lakeside has tried to partner high schools with similar problems of practice in the interest of having schools collaborate around the next level of work. In this way, partner schools can dive deeper into the possible sources of the instructional problems they share, and share resources and information as they address those problems. In some cases, paired schools may be able to share professional development and make specific commitments to supporting one another.

### Provide educators with language and a framework for considering race.

Finally, just as educators sometimes need educational frameworks to help them give language and meaning to classroom tasks (think Bloom's Taxonomy, for example), educators will need language or frameworks to help them make sense of racialized classroom patterns ("most of the kids in the AP class were white girls") or about race more generally ("the black-white achievement gap"). As this case has shown, educators will not generally talk about or deal with race directly during instructional rounds. As we saw in chapter 8, there are existing texts and frameworks that may help provide language and a process for supporting these conversations.

# Does Rounds Work?

## The View from Lakeside

At a time when school improvement efforts are measured almost solely by test scores, it was a real leap of faith for the office that supports high schools in the Lakeside Public Schools district to use the rounds process as a vehicle to meet the goals outlined in the superintendent's agenda. The question "Does rounds work?" in the context of this testing environment was repeatedly put forth to all of us and, at times, made us question the value of rounds. But as we discovered, to understand whether rounds "works," you have to do rounds repeatedly over time. As we finish our second year of rounds at Lakeside, we can confidently say that we have facilitated seventy-one district rounds to date, observed over eleven hundred classrooms, and have twenty high schools at various phases of facilitating school-based rounds. The question "Does rounds work?" no longer comes up.

This transition did not happen overnight. In particular, managing this transition means that we've had to increase our own capacity for supporting student learning, observe closely for changes in the professional culture of the system, and anticipate new challenges along the way. In Lakeside, we've used the following three questions to reflect on our rounds work of the past two years:

- What difference is rounds making in the effort to create the organizational capacity to support student learning?
- What changes do we see in schools as a result of rounds so far?
- What new challenges lie ahead?

**What difference is rounds making in the effort to create the organizational capacity to support student learning?**

Lakeside decided to use rounds as a process to create a collaborative culture and build a common language across schools. In our effort to build a professional collaborative culture, we had to battle a culture in which school leaders were positioned to compete against each other and, overwhelmed with improving their own students' test scores, did not have the capacity to collectively solve problems. At the same time, some of our high schools face much greater challenges than other schools and receive disproportionate populations of middle school repeaters (part of our promotion policy), students with special needs, and English language learners. Yet we measure school success using the same assessment data for all schools. As a result, many of our leaders work under the fear of having their schools shut down. In fact, five schools closed as we began our second year of rounds.

How do we build a collaborative culture in which leaders are focused on the learning of all students within the system, given these inequities? We started by collectively analyzing the data. To collaborate and trust one another, we had to mutually agree upon the inequities. And as a system, we had to move from judging leaders according to assessment data to cooperating on the basis of what we now know about these inequities. When we visited one another with a focus on a problem of practice as part of rounds, leaders began to shift their thinking from the individual school site to the whole system. Many offered suggestions on ways to even the playing field among schools and have come to look to one another to solve problems.

Another real tension that existed when we set out to implement rounds at Lakeside was in building capacity at school sites to facilitate internal rounds while visiting each school just once a year—essentially doing what sometimes felt like a onetime event at each school. It has taken a full two years for there to be an authentic, constant interplay between the larger system and the patterns of individual school learning. We will need to continue to create opportunities for purposeful interchange between the system and school-based instructional patterns emerging during instructional rounds.

Through rounds we were able to focus intensively on the actual academic tasks that students are being asked to do in our classrooms. In our effort to focus on rigor, we use Bloom's Taxonomy as an analytical tool in building our common language about the work being expected from our students. Our system pattern, as we unfortunately realized, was that most classroom tasks, including our more prestigious schools, were at the *remembering* and *understanding* levels, with some opportunities for application of knowledge. We had focused so long on writing clear high-level objectives and lesson plans that we were missing the observation of the most critical piece that surfaces when doing rounds during the prediction phase: What will students know and be able to do as a result of participating in the task? In other words, we found great disparity between what we call the stated task and the enacted task. We had spent so much time in the past training teachers to write high-level objectives and to use the objectives as a means to provide evaluative feedback that we missed the entire boat—what the students are actually doing. This is not to say we do not have talented teachers providing students with opportunities for higher-order thinking; this was a system-wide problem of practice. As a system, we had to understand why we were persistently asking our students to participate in lower-order thinking in the context of the central tenet of rounds—the idea that task predicts performance.

The peak learning for the system came from uncovering our misconceptions about student learning. Many of our students have not attained some of the necessary skills that high school teachers think are necessary for success. In a well-intentioned effort to remediate this problem, teachers focus mostly on providing students with opportunities to attain the basic skills that teachers deem necessary to complete higher-level content-based tasks. The mistaken belief is that students with low-level skills cannot manage higher-order, content-based tasks and should not be asked to do so until they have mastered the basics. As we found, students in our classrooms are continuously practicing basic skills in an effort to prepare themselves for high-level tasks someday. The question now is how do we negotiate learning for students with low-level skills who at the same time have the capacity for high-level thinking? Providing a perpetual basic skills curriculum is not the answer and only produces a system in which teachers learn to have low expectations for these students. *For student learning to change, the adults need to change first.*

The underlying learning theory, as we came to understand, is what we have come to call ladder versus web thinking. The basic concept is that some educators view Bloom's Taxonomy as a hierarchy of skills with steps, as in rungs on a ladder, until the learner reaches the top rung. In contrast, web thinking views Bloom Taxonomy's as nonlinear with opportunities for students to enter learning at any place within the web and not necessarily at the remembering (lowest) level of the taxonomy. We found that this distinction places teachers at different places in terms of offering high-levels tasks. For reasons previously mentioned, the ladder approach contributes to the pattern observed for the school system. Web thinkers, on the other hand, state they are not offering higher-level tasks, because, simply put, they don't know how. Rounds and the rigor course have given us a platform to have these conversations and construct the next level of work together. We have done this through consistent analysis of tasks and the thinking involved in completing the task. The real work is in creating the necessary structures for teachers to analyze practice in the effort to improve student learning.

### What changes do we see in schools as a result of rounds so far?

As we transferred some of the responsibility for the instructional rounds process to individual schools, we saw many shifts in the development of an ongoing professional culture. We learned that a school cannot institute rounds as a new initiative on its own, but that it needs to tie rounds to the professional development needs and school improvement plans in a cyclical process in which each informs the next. The most powerful outcome for schools instituting rounds has been in teachers' ability to identify their own professional development needs on the basis of their own facilitation and consistent participation in rounds. Teachers and leaders alike have identified this bottom-up approach as having a much greater impact on teacher implementation as a result of professional development participation. It has transformed school cultures from one in which an administrator evaluates and provides professional development recommendations with little follow-up, to observation of practice and next-level-of-work recommendations, with teachers leading the actual professional development. By noticing and using the strengths of teachers, we have all learned to value the knowledge that already exists in our schools.

During our second year of rounds, we worked with the rigor course participants in developing a *rounds → inquiry → rounds* approach. We were interested in providing teachers with opportunities to research and develop an inquiry cycle focused on a course of study aligned with their problems of practice. School-based networks have participated in rounds, engaged in a six-week course of study, and conducted rounds in a continuous cycle.

By now, we all have had the experience of observing the same students in various classrooms and changing our own initial perceptions. Just recently, I was facilitating rounds at a high school and noticed a student in a math class who seemed completely shut down. While other students had their notebooks opened, individually answered whole-class teacher questions, and solved procedural problems in their notebooks, this student sat quietly. In my mind I thought about how we might get this student back—how could we help him not fail? When we observed this same student in his history class playing *WWII Jeopardy*, the teacher announced that he and another student could not be on the same team, because it would be an unfair advantage. I watched this student lead his small group and offer many answers to win the challenges. His demeanor had changed; his face lit up—he was excited. I had made up my own internal story about this student, and this story changed within fifteen minutes of my first observation. We need to continue to notice how students are engaging in tasks and analyze the tasks they engage in. Rounds offers teachers opportunities to see their own students in other classrooms behaving in different ways and performing a range of academic tasks: there is no greater tool in changing belief systems.

While doing rounds, I have collected written teacher feedback after the rounds visits, conducted surveys of rigor course participants, and led various discussions regarding the value of rounds. The school-based organizational themes that emerged from rounds include the identification of the following opportunities: collect authentic, meaningful data; discuss school problems of practice; observe the daily tasks and interactions between teachers and students; appropriate best practices; and construct the next level of work together. Teachers describe rounds as a reflective process that is grounded in observing their colleagues and students and that impacts the teachers' practice without their feeling evaluated. They report shifts in thinking regarding the types and levels of academic tasks Lakeside needs to offer students, feeling a sense of mutual accountability with colleagues and engaging in deep and instructive conversations about how to improve student learning. Schools that have instituted rounds report developing a common language about instruction and learning new, effective teaching strategies. The rounds patterns have changed in schools that have implemented rounds; we no longer view lower-order thinking as the predominant task patterns that students participate in, but see spectrum patterns that include higher-order thinking. Educators at Lakeside believe rounds requires adults to do the kinds of cognitively demanding work that they wish their students would do and to share a commitment to the rounds process at their respective schools.

### What new challenges lie ahead?

You may like them. You will see. You may like them in a tree.
—Dr. Seuss, *Green Eggs and Ham*

While most feedback regarding participation in the rounds process has been positive, involving adults in rigorous work that is complex, ambiguous, thought-provoking, and personally or emotionally challenging has its share of tribulations.

We have had folks walk out, cry, and just plain refuse to participate. And we have learned that the two central reasons that teachers do not offer students high-level tasks are because either the teachers believe that the students aren't ready or the teachers don't know how. Changing belief systems is a difficult task in a system where some believe "these kids can't do that." It also takes time. Rounds has been the perfect platform for these discussions, and we need to continue to recruit our talented educators to build capacity in leading these conversations. While we have spent much of our time analyzing tasks, we need to spend more of our time working with teachers in designing and carrying out opportunities for students to participate in high-level tasks. This is our next level of work.

As we close our second year of rounds and we notice high schools at different levels of the rounds work, we are thinking about how to differentiate the support we provide from our central office. We also want to know how we can use the existing collaborative network structures to share in the support. In essence, how can we all share in the responsibility for one another's learning?

Finally, there is no doubt we need to think more deeply about processes to engage educators in discussions of existing achievement gaps during instructional rounds. We need to know *how* to have a dialogue when we notice that a special education class is composed of six male African American students or that an AP class has all Asian students, two African American females, and one African American male. All of these factors impact our relationship with schooling; we know that all students can and should have access to rigorous instruction and learning. We need to learn from our schools that have closed achievement gaps—we have such schools right here. The challenge for us is in adopting the protocols necessary to respond when the difficult conversations come up, rather than just changing the subject.

My colleagues and I used to think that when a Harvard doctoral student asks to follow you around for a year to do research—you should run like hell. Our collective experience with researchers has mostly been that they come, they steal, they critique, and, to top it all off, they make the big bucks from the book they write based on the work of folks doing the real work. This would not be a mutually beneficial relationship, and we were prepared to run.

Despite my fears, I decided to meet with John and share my feelings up front. Together we set the parameters of our working relationship, and he agreed to debrief with me once a week to further our learning through rounds. We asked

John not to withhold knowledge when he saw us making mistakes along this evolving road of rounds. He became part of the work, and we all came to rely on him for guidance and support. He did not interfere; instead, he asked the right questions at the right time. A year later, we still look to him when we come upon situations that elude us. I used to hear, "Who needs Harvard?" Now I hear, "We should talk to John about that." Now we think that practitioner and researcher can have a mutually beneficial relationship, and this, indeed, is a culture shift for all of us. We admire and thank John for generously donating all of his author's proceeds of this book to support the instructional rounds work at Lakeside.

Rounds at Lakeside has been an unbalancing act. I thank the educators who participated in our rigor course, and my coteachers who worked so hard to make the course a good learning experience for us all. I also thank the academic superintendent of high schools and the assistant academic superintendent for letting this work simmer and for teaching us the meaning of *learning the work by doing the work.*

> *Sofia Uson,*
> *instructional coach for high schools*
> *and instructional rounds facilitator,*
> *Lakeside Public Schools*

# NOTES

## Introduction

1. Throughout this book, the names of educators, schools, and the school system have been altered as part of my agreement with the school district. In some places, I have slightly altered excerpts or documents to protect the identity of the educators with whom I spoke.

2. The idea of disrupting typical patterns of interaction comes from two main areas of research: disruptive technology and social network analysis. The first is probably best represented by Clayton Christensen, Curtis W. Johnson, and Michael B. Horn, *Disrupting Class: How Disruptive Innovation Will Change the Way the World Learns* (New York: McGraw-Hill, 2008). The second is a method for documenting and describing the informal relationships (ties) and structure that exists in schools and that influence the flow of information in school organizations. See, for example, Alan J. Daly, ed., *Social Network Theory and Educational Change* (Cambridge, MA: Harvard Education Press, 2010).

3. Judith Warren Little, "The Persistence of Privacy: Autonomy and Initiative in Teachers' Professional Relations," *Teachers College Record* 91, no. 4 (1990): 509–536, gives a wonderful account of this phenomenon.

4. Richard Hackman, *Leading Teams: Setting the Stage for Great Performances* (Boston: Harvard Business School Publishing, 2002), is a good example of how we'll think about the importance of teams—and especially effective ways to manage teams—in this book. Chris Argyris, Donald Schön, and Peter Senge have long written about how organizations learn; in this book we'll focus on the learning of the system writ large, rather than the performance of particular schools or student groups. This focus on the system draws heavily on their ways of thinking about organizational learning.

   See, for example, Chris Argyris and Donald Schön, *Organizational Learning: A Theory of Action Perspective* (Reading, MA: Addison-Wesley, 1978); and Peter Senge, *The Art and Practice of the Learning Organization* (New York: Doubleday, 1990).

5. There are several good resources for the concept of classroom tasks, but I'll draw heavily on Walter Doyle, "Academic Work," *Review of Educational Research* 53,

no. 2, 159–199; and Elizabeth A. City, Richard F. Elmore, Sarah E. Fiarman, and Lee Teitel, *Instructional Rounds in Education: A Network Approach to Improving Teaching and Learning* (Cambridge, MA: Harvard Education Press, 2009).

6. Several of Richard Elmore's papers are helpful for understanding how the principal of reciprocity is actually a particular type of lateral accountability among educators in a school or system. ("Building a New Structure for School Leadership," Albert Shanker Institute, Washington, DC, winter 2000; and "The Price of Accountability: Want to Improve Schools? Invest in the People Who Work in Them," *Results [National Staff Development Council]*, November 2002). Both papers are cited in City et al., *Instructional Rounds in Education*, in the context of introducing the principal of reciprocity, which I subsequently problematize in this book.

## Chapter 1

1. As explained in the introduction, I have used pseudonyms for the school system, schools, and educators throughout this book, as part of my agreement with the school district. Some quotes have been slightly altered, to protect the identity of the educators with whom I spoke.

2. Lakeside is now revising the rigor framework. Currently, the rigor document is quite static. As a result of Lakeside's discussions with experts in the field, the school district is trying to adopt a more developmental framework for rigor, one that articulates multiple stages of growth in several domains.

3. Elizabeth A. City, Richard F. Elmore, Sarah E. Fiarman, and Lee Teitel, *Instructional Rounds in Education: A Network Approach to Improving Teaching and Learning* (Cambridge, MA: Harvard Education Press, 2009), use the term *network* to describe a group that shares a common rounds practice. These networks can take a variety of configurations and might have members from one district or from several school systems in a cross-district network. Different network configurations serve different purposes. The Lakeside network initially comprised all thirty-eight high school principals and the Lakeside staff who support the high schools, including an academic superintendent and special education administrators who work primarily with the high schools.

4. Dave is one of twenty-five teachers in the district who attend a district-sponsored graduate-level course that they affectionately call Rigor Class. Most of the teachers and principals enrolled in the class also have some responsibility for facilitating rounds at their schools. Sofia is one of the course instructors. More on this later, but the course is one way that Lakeside Public Schools began to try to make

connections between the rounds practice, professional development, and other improvement processes happening across the system.

5. City et al., *Instructional Rounds*, use the term *instructional core* as part of a set of broader principles about what kinds of school improvement work is the most high-leverage. In short, they argue that focusing classroom observations on the interaction of teachers and students in the presence of content has the greatest potential to inform teachers' practice. In addition, they provide a set of seven principles about the instructional core. For more reading on this idea, one helpful piece is David Hawkins, "I, Thou and It," in *The Informed Vision: Essays on Learning and Human Nature* (New York: Agathon Books, 1974), 49–62.

## Chapter 3

1. As I mentioned in the introduction, Chris Argyris and Donald Schön, *Organizational Learning: A Theory of Action Perspective* (Reading, MA: Addison-Wesley, 1978), is helpful for understanding theories of action and the ideas of single-loop and double-loop learning. The models I develop at the end of this chapter for incorporating the rounds process into other parts of the school system draw heavily on their work.

2. There are a number of helpful papers on the concepts of self-efficacy and collective efficacy, but one that seems to apply directly here is Albert Bandura, "Perceived Self-Efficacy in Cognitive Development and Functioning," *Educational Psychologist* 28, no. 2 (1993): 117–148, which outlines concepts of both self-efficacy and collective efficacy.

3. One potential weakness to this approach is that teachers could initially view it as a process whereby the system evaluates the quality or impact of the professional development being provided in the district. Rounds could do that for a system, but probably only after many months of regular practice with rounds, and I would still argue that this isn't the purpose of the process in the first place. Facilitators and leaders would need to emphasize regularly the learning stance of rounds; otherwise, a model like this could potentially send the wrong messages to educators.

## Chapter 4

1. Elizabeth A. City, Richard F. Elmore, Sarah E. Fiarman, and Lee Teitel, *Instructional Rounds in Education: A Network Approach to Improving Teaching and Learning* (Cambridge, MA: Harvard Education Press, 2009), provide these as the general features of a strong problem of practice.

## Chapter 6

1. Robert L. Linn, "Accountability: Responsibility and Reasonable Expectations," presidential address, American Educational Research Association, Chicago, April 23, 2003; A. Porter and M. Chester, "Building a High-Quality Assessment and Accountability Program: The Philadelphia Example," paper presented at a Brookings Institution Conference, Washington, DC, May 2001. See also Susan H. Fuhrman and Richard F. Elmore, *Redesigning Accountability Systems for Education* (New York: Columbia University, Teacher's College Press, 2004).

## Chapter 7

1. See, for example, Jal Mehta, "The Transformation of American Educational Policy, 1980–2001: Ideas and the Rise of Accountability Politics," Ph.D. diss., Harvard University, Cambridge, MA.

2. Richard Elmore has written about lateral accountability in education. In particular, he argues with others that at some point in the process, the work of school improvement must include the giving away of authority, for example, from the central office to schools, from principals to groups of teachers. The purpose of this transfer is to allow for the development of more collegial commitments that replace typical hierarchical arrangements of large school systems. Of course, the network arrangement of rounds is built heavily on this idea, but it seemed important to mention it here.

3. My colleagues in the Instructional Rounds Institute at the Harvard Graduate School of Education—Richard Elmore, Liz City, Lee Teitel, Stefanie Reinhorn, and Tim O'Brien—are currently thinking about how to support school systems in this transition. Listening to their conversations about this has been incredibly instructive for me and played a role in how I presented some of the information in parts 1 and 2 of this book. In particular, they helped me see some of Lakeside's problems as developmental ones, with both technical and cultural components.

## Chapter 8

1. The typical markers used to identify young people in most schools are particularly blunt and poor descriptors. Most school districts are required by states to assign students to categories called black, white, Latino, Asian, and so forth. However, these terms mask a huge diversity of ethnicities and identities that matter for this discussion. In this chapter, I use the racial identities that are typically used to identify students (and teachers) in this school system, but the reader should keep in mind some of the ways in which these racial markers might be insufficient.

2. John B. Diamond, "Cultivating a School-Based Discourse That Emphasizes Teachers' Responsibility for Student Learning," in *Everyday Antiracism: Concrete Ways to Successfully Navigate the Relevance of Race in School*, ed. Mica Pollock (New York: New Press, 2008).

3. The idea of "doing race" comes from a book of the same title: Hazel Rose Markus and Paula M. L. Moya, eds., *Doing Race* (New York: W. W. Norton & Company, 2010). The book contains twenty-one essays targeted mostly to undergraduates. It has been mentioned to me repeatedly by educators since I began working on this book.

## Chapter 9

1. Paul Hager, "Conceptions of Learning and Understanding Learning at Work," *Studies in Continuing Education* 26, no. 1 (2004).

# ACKNOWLEDGMENTS

Liz City, Richard Elmore, Tim O'Brien, Stefanie Reinhorn, and Lee Teitel are my colleagues at the Harvard Graduate School of Education. I learn more from teaching with them than I do in any other part of my professional life. They have contributed a tremendous amount of thinking to this book, but any mistakes, errors, or omissions are my own.

Caroline Chauncey and the team at Harvard Education Press provided consistent, effective feedback along the way. I learned more from Caroline about my writing than at any other time in graduate school.

This book is adapted in part from my dissertation submitted for the degree of Doctor of Education to the Harvard Graduate School of Education. The feedback and guidance that Professors Richard Elmore, Jal Mehta, and John Diamond provided during that process have subsequently improved this book.

Dr. Margaret McDevitt and my colleagues in Lowell, Massachusetts, were willing to learn instructional rounds with me. I am so grateful for that support and friendship. There were a number of other educators who were also helpful along the way, including Mark Church, Cathy Meyer-Looze, Rick Vandermolen, Jayne Mohr, and Pam Alifieri of the Traverse City Schools in Traverse City, Michigan. David Shepherd, Jan McClure, and the educators of Ballarat Clarendon College in Ballarat, New South Wales, Australia, also played a helpful role in the development of this book. Judith DeWoskin, of Ann Arbor, MI, was my first mentor.

I am grateful to my family and friends for their support. Chris Dombrowski, Alexander Deussen, Tobias Lawrence, Nick Popoff, Bret Shrader, and Matt Welch provided a consistent reminder of the importance of my friends. My brother Luke is a school principal in Wuxi, China, who helped me think through parts of this book—and whom I miss dearly. Finally, I thank my partner, Liliana, for her patience and love.

All of the author's proceeds will be donated to the school district profiled in this book, to support the professional learning of educators.

# ABOUT THE AUTHOR

**John E. Roberts** is a 2012 graduate of the Harvard Graduate School of Education. He has served as a middle school teacher in Michigan and was assistant director of the Lowell Middlesex Academy Charter School, in Lowell, Massachusetts, from 2003 to 2006. More recently, John has taught and facilitated for professional education programs, including the Instructional Rounds Institute at the Harvard Graduate School of Education. He was a contributing author to Katherine Merseth's *Inside Urban Charter Schools* (Harvard Education Press) in 2009. He currently lives in Washington, DC.

# INDEX